GEORGIA FOOTBALL MEMORIES:

50 YEARS OF STATE - SPONSORED ANTAGONISM

A COLLECTION OF MEMORIES

STEVE ANTHONY

"Georgia Football Memories: 50 Years of State-Sponsored Antagonism," by Steve Anthony. ISBN 978-1-62137-933-1 (softcover); 978-1-62137-934-8 (eBook).

Cover image courtesy Busara/Shutterstock.com for editorial, non-fiction use. All internal images courtesy and copyright of Steve Anthony.

Published 2016 by Virtualbookworm.com Publishing Inc., P.O. Box 9949, College Station, TX 77842, US. ©2016, Steve Anthony.

TABLE OF CONTENTS

INTRODUCTION

FOR A BOY GROWING UP in the southern United States during the middle of the 20th century—the forties (before and after the war), the fifties and most of the sixties—if he was into sports, he was exposed to football. In an almost equal amount, he was exposed to baseball, but that was more to fill the day and burn energy in the summer. (Its nickname is not "The National Pastime" for nothing!) Basketball hardly had a following at all. These were the "pre-Pete Maravich" days, which is another story altogether. But let's not digress!

Of course, when I say "southern United States," I am referring only to the states of Georgia, Alabama, Mississippi, Tennessee, South Carolina, Louisiana and, to a lesser extent, Arkansas, North Carolina and Kentucky—to an even lesser extent Texas and Oklahoma. They were not then nor are they now part of the "southeast," but Texas, nevertheless, was very much into football. The cultures of Texas and Oklahoma are different from the rest of the southern states, yet I must concede that they do have similarities. As a whole, though, the Southeast is a culture, region and mindset all to itself.

High school football, and college football in selected areas, was followed religiously during that time. It had a following not only from the youngsters but from the town folks as well. It was followed almost exclusively through the radio or in person, and it remained this way until the mid-sixties. Football was not the best game in town—it was the only game. It was followed at the college level by those who could pick up a game on the radio or lived in the college town, but this was possible only for the chosen few. There were no professional sports in the South then, so college sports were all you had past high school. It was more than enough. Following high school football in this region created a natural flow to college. I am sure I do not have to expound on the cultural embrace of Friday night football in high schools throughout the South. How many high school stadiums in other regions of the country had seating capacities of 5,000 or more when the town's population would be not more than, say, 20,000?

Football was not for everyone, though—you either embraced this game or you did not. For those who did embrace it, it was more than a game. It was a microcosm of the southern mind, culture and attitude. That is why most of us embraced it. It was part of our mindset. It represented what we thought we were.

Love of a particular team naturally resulted from the love of the game. You *had* to pick a team. If you liked football and were in a conversation about football where they were talking about team "X", and you did not have a favorite team "Y", you were excluded from the conversation.

So here in Georgia, that meant picking between University of Georgia and Georgia Tech. My family members were then, and are now, Georgia Bulldog fans. My father had not gone to college (although he was accepted into Notre Dame), much less gone to UGA. But UGA was the biggest school then, as now[1]. It was the flagship and also the linchpin for so much of agricultural Georgia. The state truly was different then. Sadly for many, that Georgia no longer exists.

Let's contrast UGA with Georgia Tech. Tech was in Atlanta, and it taught courses most people did not take, classes that were "foreign" to them. One of my Dad's dearest lifelong friends went there, so he knew more about Tech than most. It was seen as a small, elitist school (although public, not private). In short, it was everything that was opposite "rural Georgia" (a redundant phrase at the time). And so, my father was "naturally" a UGA Bulldog supporter. I never questioned the reasons for this, much less the logic behind it.

---

[1] UGA was the biggest college *on one campus*. Many universities and colleges in Georgia have more than one location but count the total attendance as one total. Recent mergers have added to this "new math." I am sure that if this is read 20 years from now, this dynamic will be much different. But in that era, that was the size of it! Pun intended.

My brother was the first in our family to go to college, and he picked UGA. He started in 1963 and graduated in the fall of 1967. Why in the fall? He wanted to squeeze in one extra football season! Later his two sons and one of my two sons graduated from UGA. I received a scholarship to another school, West Georgia College, so I went there.

Around the time when I was in my early teens (mid-1960s), I had been indoctrinated into the "whys" and "wherefores" of being *for* UGA and *against* Ga. Tech. Why you were for one team or another was somewhat equally distributed by motivation.

In 1961, at ten years of age, I went to my first Georgia football game. It was against Auburn in Athens, and it was also the first time I saw UGA in person. Two things stood out to me about that game. We saw our hometown (Rome) priest in the stands. He had played at Georgia, but I thought it interesting that a priest was going to things like football games! Secondly, my brother and I fell in love with the bulldog—the animal and the team. We loved bulldogs so much that we badgered our Dad until he bought us an English Bulldog for our pet. And so I had, and later *became*, a bulldog!

That Auburn game was the only game I went to until 1966. My brother, of course, went to all the home games and some of the away ones (although I am not sure my Dad knew about all of those), but I was shut out. I could follow them on the radio and the "once in a blue moon" telecast (UGA vs. Alabama, 1965, comes immediately to mind), but not in person.

There are a couple of things to remember about that time period to keep this in context. Tech was a powerhouse under Bobby Dodd through most of the 1950s, while Georgia had a "down decade" in the fifties under Wallace Butts (with the exception of the Tarkenton Era). Then they floundered worse under Johnny Griffith in the early sixties. Griffith had taken over for Wallace Butts in 1961 because the program was in duress and turmoil. Griffith only lasted three years. He inherited a mess and could not pull out of it.

In my career later in life, I got to know Coach Griffith pretty well. And there is not a nicer, more gentlemanly man that I have ever known. This is one example of life being put into proper context.

But let's get back to the story. As a result of Griffith's firing, Georgia's Athletic Director, Joel Eaves, hired a new young coach from Auburn in November of 1963, Vincent Joseph Dooley. Eaves was an Auburn alum also—just one of the many connections between the two schools.

Tech had beaten Georgia in 1961, 1962, and 1963—three very formative years for a young boy. Because of those beatings, I could have said, "Why in the world are we *for* the Bulldogs? I want a winner." Or I could have stayed true and thought, *I am for them regardless of the outcome, and I will always be for them, not just when they win.* I did the latter. My own personal thought process, though not grounded in reason or logic but comforting nonetheless, was that my beliefs were correct regardless of what happened on the field. Looking back now, I believed what I believed based on what I would hear and read. It certainly was not based on first-hand knowledge, as you can imagine for a 10-12-year-old.

I was conditioned to believe, not by any one person but by the culture I was living in, that UGA represented rural Georgia, which was the *real* Georgia. Atlanta was something different altogether. Let me add here that it was not just about race; it was also about the "big city," the traffic, the lack of open spaces. These things are attributes typically seen in the American rural versus urban debate. It was "hassles" versus "no hassles." Of course, that too was mostly fiction. But if someone had never been to Atlanta and had only heard these things about the city, then how were they to know it was not true?

UGA represented and was followed by those who had little, worked hard with their hands, and many times had little education to fall back on. Back then, before the sixties, less than 10% of the population graduated from college. (In 2015, the percentage was up to only 35!) UGA represented the essence of the state; whereas, Tech represented something else—"the elites," or so we were conditioned to believe. UGA represented a goal for anyone who wanted a college degree, though most did not meet that goal. Tech's curriculum was for some other type of person, and many times that person was a student from another state!

Let me quickly add that most of the political and business elites of that time period did, in fact, graduate from UGA. The non-elites are not the only ones who followed UGA rather than Tech.

We were also conditioned to believe that all Tech people thought they were better than those who went to Athens. It was "rural life and agricultural" versus "science and math." To me and others, Tech represented big city life, the elite of society. It represented everything with which I had no contact; whereas, UGA represented everything with which I *did* have contact. Plus, who even uses engineering and technology? (That's a joke, Techies!) Let me put it another way. The Georgia Farm Bureau and the importance of the Cooperative Extension Service operating out of UGA were not something anybody at Tech even knew about, much less appreciated. This was such an ethereal concept at that point in time. Tech had no connection to the affairs of our state, so we were led to believe. But to some extent, it was true.

In other words, the mentality was "us against the world" because "*we* had little and *they* had a lot, *and* they were the reason for this imbalance." This is what we were conditioned to believe.

The truth is, Tech *did* look down on UGA, for no reason other than they thought a science degree or something similar was better than a liberal arts, education or agriculture degree. At that time, I was not aware that most elected officials in Georgia, if they went to college, had gone to Athens (Jimmy Carter being the exception). I would also come to see things much differently later in life, and I realized a lot of what I had thought or been led to believe was incorrect. (A lot—not everything!) I have even lived in downtown Atlanta for over twenty years, and I love it. I'll go more into those points later. This is just to give younger readers, or those from other regions of the country, or those who have not followed the sociological aspects of college football (and there are many!) a compass with which to navigate this concept of southern football culture.

One last thought. There is always a lot of chatter, especially when Tech is down, about how important "this game" is relative to the rest of UGA's schedule. It is and shall always be the most important. Why? There are many reasons.

First, it establishes superiority in the state for recruiting, media coverage, bragging rights and more. Secondly, in every state where there is an in-state rival, you *want* to win. It doesn't matter if there is an imbalance. The third reason this game is the most important is because there are so many divided loyalties. Why would you not care for the one you have to live with every day? We do not come into contact with a Gator or Tiger or Vol fan every day—we do, however, have frequent contact with Tech fans.

You need three things for a rivalry—similarity (both are in Georgia, players come from the same high schools, etc.), proximity (they're only 60 miles apart) and history (no need to elaborate here). You can have more than one rivalry, as you know. I am primarily talking about which school is the biggest rival. Another way to measure the pecking order of teams and their rivalries is by asking the question, "Do you get pleasure from their failure or misfortune?" That is called "schadenfreude." A corollary that is sometimes seen but maybe not as much is "gluckschmerz," displeasure from the other side's good fortune. If you have those feelings for Tech or UGA then you can safely say that yes, it is a rivalry, and it is the biggest. It is 2014-2015 at the time I am writing this book, and, as you know, Tech won in 2014. All of a sudden, some UGA fans considered it a rivalry. All it takes is one defeat. So you decide…Is it a rivalry? Is it the biggest for each school?

With this scenario as a backdrop, I started a journey that I had no idea would lead to where it has led and which became sort of a "cause célèbre." As we entered 2015, I was on the verge of attending my 50th straight Tech-Georgia game.

This offering is a remembrance of that experience, with comments and anecdotes on each game. I am sure other fans have had similar experiences, but this is uniquely mine. I have read of one gentleman who is a Tech fan who has gone to, at last count,

71 straight UGA-Tech games. Congrats—I know that will not be matched.

As far as I could research, there is no other printed (or electronic) book detailing this fifty-year period. There is, of course, *Clean, Old-Fashioned Hate*, which has some of these years included in it. Other books have highlighted games, but there are none that cover every game, good and bad. This is the period of *the* modern era in this rivalry.

It may be hard to believe, but my stories here are mostly spawned from memory. I did double-check my facts and statistics to make sure the 'ole memory is not deceiving me. It is funny that I can remember more details from the earlier games that I went to when I was young. The older I got, with a family, job and other items of life taking up my brain space and emotions, the less detail I could remember. So I double-checked. And of course, now you can find some of the games on YouTube. I really enjoyed watching them again while doing this "research."

Also, I have tried my best to recount the feelings I had at the time of the game rather than from the perspective of "looking back." You should be able to clearly imagine my reactions and feelings as a teenager rather than as an adult, older adult and finally senior citizen!

After reading each year's accounts, you will feel like you were there, a feeling which can only come from me having been there. I do not have all the old tickets. Sometimes I was "allowed" in, and sometimes I even paid a gatekeeper! Sometimes at Tech I was almost thrown out! Sometimes I had a pass for the field. The fact is, until I was forced to start getting in on my own, I relied on my Dad or some other adult to secure admission. As a result, for the first few years I just viewed this as a good game to go to because I was able to get in. During my college years, it was pretty much the same. Sometime during that period I realized I had gone to every game since 1966. By the time I got out of college and started law school in 1974, I knew I just *had* to continue to go to the Tech game every year. I thought, *I'm heading into ten straight years of going! Pretty neat. Let's see how many I can get in.* Eventually, I wanted to go because of what it *was*, regardless of having a streak. This is really a by-product of the big rivalry.

I wish I could fabricate some dramatic stories about how some years I did not know if I would make it, how some years I was on death's bed. But somewhat amazingly, that never happened. It really only took my commitment and desire to go to the game. I was lucky enough to have a job and career that kept me in Georgia. In years that I was very busy, or when the team was relatively bad, or simply as I got older and going to games became harder, I knew that come hell or high water, I *would* go to the Tech–Georgia game, if no other. All else in life during that weekend took second place to the need to be at the game. My wife and daughters-in-law wondered about my sanity. This game is always during Thanksgiving week, so when the games were on Thursday, it wrecked (no pun intended!!!) the family gatherings! When things were tough in my life, going to the game served as a comfort to me, and I always felt better because of it.

I started putting these thoughts down on paper in 2014, so the 2014 game is written in the present tense. Then, of course, I waited until the 2015 game week arrived to finish writing. Some reflections are written as an on-going narrative over time.

If, by chance, any of you reading this are not into sports but for some reason are reading, I do not expect you to understand—that is why we are called "FANatics." It is what it is.

Enjoy.

PRELUDE

FOR THOSE OF YOU coming to the party late, from another part of the country or who are just now coming of age, let me give you a little background.

Georgia Tech and the University of Georgia are both public institutions of higher learning in Georgia's university system. Both are supported by state tax dollars, grants, relatively few federal dollars, private donations, etc. The state tax dollars are collected by the state and allocated by the state. The athletics operations, however, are totally funded by any and every source *other* than state dollars. And, as with most universities, the profitability of the football program provides most of the dollars, directly and indirectly, to the other sports. I mention this because for some reason many people years ago, I guess due to the school's curriculum, assumed Tech was a private university. Even Larry Munson thought that well into the 1970s.

From its inception until the 1940s, UGA had the upper hand in most sports. Both schools were small and relatively poor, but UGA was the flagship university and had more alumni overall, especially alumni who stayed in the state. After the war (World War II, that is), things changed some. There were too many changes to recount here. For my purposes, I tell you that one of the changes was Tech getting a new coach, Bobby Dodd. This change elevated them for a sustained period to a level they had really not previously enjoyed. UGA had a good coach then as well, Wallace Butts, and several all-time great players. But even though UGA was great, Tech had gotten a lot better and caught up.

By the fifties, Georgia's success had dropped while Tech stayed strong. That brings us to the 1960s. As I mentioned in the introduction, Dooley quickly changed the scenario, winning his first five games against Tech. Parity, at the very least, had been restored.

However, as you will see, by the 1990s and into the new century, all things football related started changing, as did many other things in society, because of the powerful, financial effect of TV. In the early sixties, UGA's enrollment was about 4,000. Tech's was about 1,800-2,000. Tech even had to "import" co-eds from Agnes Scott to provide cheerleaders, and many a Tech man dated the girls from there, as well as those from Emory, since there were hardly any females at Tech.

By the start of the 21st century, UGA's enrollment was around 30,000. Tech's was bumping up to 20,000, a significant jump. When you factor in TV money, wealth of alumni, as well as the sheer number of alumni, along with increased state budgeting, you see that the two universities' programs were coming closer together than ever before.

But the aftereffects of the "Herschel Era" started UGA down a path of enormous wealth in the athletic department. Tech could not keep up. What Herschel Walker has meant to the University of Georgia could fill another entire book. His influence went way beyond winning on the football field. By the middle of the first decade of the new century, UGA was well ahead of Tech in mostly all categories football and sports related. Granted, this does not mean Tech could not win on the playing field; it only means that they had to do so with less.

By the time of this writing, there is a huge gap—in resources, alumni, and money—that shows no sign of abating. That is why I and many other UGA fans and supporters feel Ga. should never lose to Tech in football. Other sports are different because of different dynamics. In football, though, it is a function of numbers, facilities and critical mass. Any time Tech wins, it is an upset. *And* it upsets us Ga. fans, especially in this day and age with this enormous gap in the afore-mentioned areas. I know many will say that's all "bull" and even worse things. Again, I am not saying that Tech will not win. They will. They just have to do more with less. Another way to say it is that UGA does less with more, hence the enormous displeasure by UGA fans.

Now obviously, one team cannot go undefeated forever, but in the abstract many of us want that to be the case. Yes, the difference between 2,000 students (Tech in 1966) and 4,000 (UGA in 1964) is not as great as the difference between twenty-something-thousand and thirty-something-thousand, but it actually is. The amount of notoriety and money that can be generated is enormous at those levels. Also, one or two victories do not make a trend. I am talking about sustained parity. For most of these years, when Tech won, it was an unpredicted victory. I can name the years Tech went in as a favorite and won in a chart at the end of the book. But here they are: 1970, 1990, 2000 (pick-um).

One final caution. This is written by a University of Georgia supporter, and I am that in every sense of the word. Money, support, comment and assistance. I have given all of those. It is written from that perspective, and it is written honestly. So those of you who lean toward Tech can expect to get mad. My opinions, my feelings and my emotions are here, and they are biased. However, as I think you will see, I try to honestly assess the games. But I am a fan of one of these teams and not the other, so this is not an even-handed account in the journalistic sense. As I said, the years covered here happen to be the majority of what can be termed the "modern era" of college football and, therefore, the modern era of this rivalry.

MY FIFTY YEARS OF FOLLOWING AND
GOING TO THE GEORGIA - GEORGIA TECH
FOOTBALL GAME, YEAR BY YEAR.

1966

THIS WAS MY MAIDEN GAME. By this time Dooley was coaching his third Tech-Ga. Game, and he had won the first two, one in Athens and one at Grant Field. This game was in Athens. My Dad had gotten tickets, and we wanted to go see a game with my brother and his girlfriend (who later became his wife). We had never done that in the three years he had been at UGA. I was, of course, excited, but this excitement was greatly enhanced by the two teams that were to play. In many ways, this was a seminal game in the series and still is, though many times it is overlooked. Coach Bobby Dodd had earlier announced that this would be his last season coaching. He was going out in style. At this point of the season, Tech was undefeated, 9-0. There were only ten regular season games back then. The Bulldogs were not bad themselves. They were 8-1 with only a one-point loss to Miami under the leadership of their All-American quarterback, George Mira. Georgia had also won the Southeastern Conference Championship that year. Tech had dropped out of the conference a few years earlier, so Georgia's conference schedule was finished. As I said, this was Coach Dooley's third season, so to be conference champs entering this game toe-to-toe with Tech had the Bulldog fans pumped like no one had seen in several decades. I, at the time, did not know or realize all this. I was just happy to be going to a big game.

The weather was great, with high sunny skies, and the press was in full coverage. Several current and future All-Americans were playing. In today's era, this would have been *the* game of the week, and ESPN's GameDay would have been there. Back then, this battle was just of interest in the South. Nationally,

Notre Dame and Michigan State were dominating the news; these two Georgia-based teams were afterthoughts. What a great game to be my first. For us, this was *real* football!

Georgia won 23-14, which was not that close. Tech was favored. They were ranked 5th coming in, and Ga. was ranked 7th after beating top-ten Florida with eventual Heisman Trophy winner Steve Spurrier as quarterback. Georgia had a stout defense with just enough offense, a coming trademark of the Dooley era.

Kent Lawrence, who went on to become a State Court judge, returned a punt for a touchdown. I remember this easily because it was one of the only times there was a cannon at the edge of the end zone that went off just as he was scoring. As he was entering the end zone, it almost blew him up! When they lined up for the extra point, Bobby Etter missed. That was why the score was 23 instead of 24.

We were in the north corner at about the five-yard line, on the lower deck (there was no upper deck then, so really, it was the *only* deck). I remember looking at the stadium so much that I did not see a lot of the plays. I did see the ones that counted. After the game was over, I remember having the feeling that "it does not get any better than this." It eventually would, but at that time I could not imagine how. Georgia had now won three straight games after losing the previous three before Dooley arrived. Vince was put on a throne by the fans and had wound up 3-0 against the great Bobby Dodd.

All of these facts made this one of the most compelling and important Tech-Ga. games of the 20th century. Of course, at that time it did not mean that to me. As time has passed, it has become more evident. Also, as a 16-year-old, I thought all games would be like this. I later find out otherwise.

Coach Dooley and Coach Dodd went on to become great friends after that up until Dodd's death.

I got to know Coach Dodd well in my job, and he would regal me with tales of college football. He also told me how he "loved" Vince; he made him a lot of money on games, and he knew he could count on Dooley to have his teams prepared almost all the time. He always bet on him when he was the underdog. Dodd was a classy guy and a great figure in Georgia annals. He, really, was the reason many people then were fans of Tech. They were not so much fans of Tech but of Dodd. I told him that once, and he actually blushed, but I think deep inside he knew and agreed.

Later in 1966, Tech went on and lost to that same Florida team in the Orange Bowl, and Georgia beat SMU in the Cotton Bowl. Georgia finished 4th that year and Tech finished 8th.

1967

THIS WAS MY FIRST GAME at Grant Field ever, and it was equally entertaining. I sat in the lower deck, east side, all by myself. I think my brother had dropped me off, and while he went and sat in his seats, I sat where they had an extra ticket: lower deck, the side where the other Ga. fans were relegated. It would be the first of many games I would attend, but it was the only one of the Tech games that I went to by myself. Again I had no pre-conceived feelings about the outcome.

This game was similar to the '66 game. Bud Carson was in his first year at Tech and Georgia had had an up and down year. They beat Auburn but lost by one point to both Houston and Florida. They only played five conference games when most of the other conference teams played six. Don't ask me why! They would finish 7-4 after losing to future coach Jim Donnan and the NC State Wolfpack in the Liberty Bowl. But when the Tech game arrived, they were ready. I remember looking around a lot at Grant field (much like the previous year in Athens) and marveling at the differences between it and Sanford Stadium. I will leave it at that!

Georgia won 21-14, and again the score was deceptive. That victory made four in a row. Vince was undefeated against Tech. So far, so good.

The weather was not as good as it was in 1966. It was not bad, but it was cloudy and threatening all day. I mention this because I remember thinking I was not dressed right if it rained (that will be a *big* topic in a later game) and contemplating if I could deal with it. I resolved at that game that it would never matter what the weather was—the Tech-Ga. game demanded attendance. That was a small sacrifice I could make for the game.

Not every game in this telling will be compelling, energetic and nail-biting. This is one of them.

I also will try not to engage in psychoanalyzing why a team won or lost, or why one had a losing streak or a winning streak. There was a lot of talk then, but it was just the garden variety you hear when someone replaces a legend. The fact is, this was about the time that leaving the SEC was catching up with Tech, and Bud Carson had to bear the brunt of that dip. (See 1968! But then read about 1969, 1970.)

This 1967 game was significantly different from the previous year in several ways. Neither team was as highly ranked, Dodd was gone and the game was relatively boring. The teams were not as good. That showed me right away that all games would not be like 1966, as I had thought and said before. I cannot remember the details, but if 25 passes were thrown by both teams during the entire game, I would be shocked. But this type of game also afforded me the opportunity to realize that it did not matter—this was Tech-Ga. The game itself was a tense affair because of the stakes.

1968

THIS IS ONE OF THE SEMINAL games in the series. Georgia wins 47-8. At the end of this book, among other things, I will rank the games based on certain critera, one of which is that which constitutes a great game: a blow-out or a close game. By any description, this was a great game for a Ga. fan.

Georgia was undefeated, with two ties against Tennessee and Houston. You may notice they had played Houston two straight years and this *just* happened to be when something called the "triple option" was coming in. Houston ran what was called a "veer" and it was as prolific an offense then as you see in the second decade of the 21st century, except that what is being run as an offense in the two-thousand teens is more like the very old single wing.

Georgia won the SEC again, and that made two times in five years that Vince had been coach.

He was back on top.

Tech meanwhile had hit the nadir and their record was 4-6. They were actually 4-2 going into the last part of the season before they lost their last four games.

This game had really overcast weather, and it may have sprinkled some. It was no matter to us Bulldog fans, however. We would have sat through a blizzard. As the game was winding down and I was absorbing all of it, I started thinking of the conundrum I mentioned earlier. Was this a "good" game or were the last two better? Was the feeling I had about this outcome better than a competitive game that would be in doubt most of the game? Remember, I was 17 then, and my conclusion was that this was a great feeling and it could not get any better. (I will change my mind later, as you will read.)

I sat in the lower section on the south side, very near the student section and band. Since Georgia had now won five in a row and it was evident early on that they would win this one, this is the game where I started to assume Ga. would always win. It was my first game where I was totally alone; my brother had graduated and I was left all to my thoughts. I had never really experienced a loss to Tech, in my mind or in my emotions. As a senior in high school, I felt that there was a natural superiority over Tech football. The glory years of Dodd were long gone, in memory if not in time.

I mention this because, as you will see in the next year, I learned a lot!

Bill Stanfill was All-American, as was Jake Scott, and Billy Payne was All-Conference, along with some others. The Ga. team was loaded with talent, but Tech was reloading. They just had not gotten enough good players yet. Carson would change that.

1969

THIS GAME IS BACK IN ATLANTA, and I am in the old horseshoe end zone in the south stands with my Dad. This is one of only two times just he and I went to this game. A treasure.

Georgia had really had an up and down year in 1969. They started out where they left off in 1968 by beating Tulane, Clemson and South Carolina (the latter two both in the ACC at that time). At that point, I recall them being on the cover of Sports Illustrated. Then they lost a close one to Ole Miss, who had a young gunslinger named Archie Manning.

Then they came back and beat Vandy and Kentucky. At that point they were 5-1. They would never win another game. They lost to eventual SEC champion Tennessee, tied with the Gators, and lost to Auburn, who also had a young quarterback of their own, Pat Sullivan, an eventual Heisman Trophy winner. (See 1971 game.)

Georgia lost to Tech 6-0.

Tech, on the other hand, had an even worse year. They went into the Ga. game with a 3-6 record. They had lost to Clemson, Tennessee, and Auburn as common opponents. They played a good game against Notre Dame but lost.

Their schedule was tougher than Georgia's, and they played the common opponents better for the most part. Nonetheless, they were an underdog, and we Ga. fans had no concern that, even though two mediocre teams were playing, Ga. was in any danger of losing. Well, Ga. did not even score. Tech barely did, and they did not even make the extra point off the touchdown. It was an all-around desultory game, except for one big point: Tech won for the first time in five years. Even with the fact that it was Tech-Ga., I found out that *the* game can be a clunker just like any other. They were two teams going nowhere. That did not make the loss any less agonizing, however.

Georgia drove the ball all day but could not put it into the end zone. It was so frustrating, but my Dad was getting a kick from watching me go through so many gyrations and emotions.

When it was over and we were in the car to drive back to Rome, he said, "I am concerned about you. You take this way too hard!"

It was a tough loss. And it was my first, in person. That's right. I had seen 5 Georgia games in a stadium and had never seen them lose. I was 18, but you would have thought I was 10. I really had some kind of feeling that Ga. would never lose to Tech as long as Vince was coaching. I felt like this was the worst life could get. I would find out the next year it could get worse, at least as far as following a college football team was concerned. Isn't it great to be young?

One further thing I found out from this game is that henceforth I would go into every game concerned about the outcome. I was interested in the fact that we could lose. By losing, I realized Ga. *could* lose. Therefore, the week before the game, I would often go through many emotions based on that year's match-up. Many of us did this, and immortalized by Dooley and Munson, we would think of every way in the world that Ga. could lose. Again, I was 18 and I really thought Ga. would always win.

1970

WE ARE BACK IN ATHENS and this year was in many ways like the year before, yet it did have differences. The main difference was that Tech was a good team, with a good record (9-3) and was a favorite against Ga. The Bulldogs, on the other hand, had a year much like 1969 (5-5).

Georgia started by losing to Tulane at the old Sugar Bowl stadium. Then they destroyed Clemson but lost to Mississippi State as well as Ole Miss in Athens. That is the game, which I attended, where Archie, a senior, got hurt and left the field. Sometime in the 3rd quarter he came jogging out, and the Ole Miss fans went nuts. You could hear a loud buzz all over the stadium...We all knew what his coming out meant. I had a sinking feeling in my stomach. Of such things legends are made.

Then Ga. beat Vandy, Kentucky, and South Carolina consecutively. Now the fun started, as always. Ga. lost to a mediocre Florida team and had to go to #4, Auburn. Guess what? Georgia won in one of the biggest upsets in their football history.

Tech, meanwhile, was storming to an 8-3 regular season record. This is one of those anomalies I pointed out from a few years ago. Tech played 11 regular season games. They lost back to back to #4 Tennessee and #8 Auburn and then later to #1 Notre Dame by three points.

They were good and were led by an All-American defensive tackle by the name of Rock Perdoni (I kid you not).

I, of course, thought in spite of all the evidence that Georgia would win. But, as I mentioned, I was worried going in and knew in the back of my mind we could lose...again! This was when I started to realize that this game was defining my existence during the week of Thanksgiving. And it still does to this day. It was really not as close as the score indicated; there was only a 10-point margin. I sat in the upper deck with some hometown friends, on the south side, and burned up in the late fall afternoon sun. By game time, Ga. was 5-4 and Tech was ranked 16th in the country. Never mind, UGA was supposed to win. There was no way the Bulldogs would lose two in a row, right? It was another one of those somewhat dull games, with not a lot of points scored by either side. Ga. only scored once. I know it sounds like the games Georgia lost were boring, and maybe you think it's just because they lost. But they really *were* boring, even at that point in time of college football. Nonetheless, it was a recipe for success for Tech.

After the game and in the following weeks, Ga. would not go to a bowl for the first time under Dooley (except in 1965), and the heat got turned up on Coach Dooley for the first time. There were calls for him to go. I was surprised and disappointed that was going on, after all he had done. On the other hand, losing two in a row gave me a new perspective on this series. No longer would I automatically feel we would win or that we were superior. Never again would I just look at the game scheduled and assume a victory. In many ways, this was a really good adjustment to deal with the realities of college football rivalries.

Final score: 7–17, Tech.

1971

THIS IS A PIVOTAL YEAR in many ways, for UGA, the SEC and college football nationally. It was, without question, the single best year in college football history.

First, most schools had a standard 11-game regular season schedule. In the SEC, a monumental shift occurred, courtesy of Bear Bryant. He had had two down years for Alabama, and got crushed by USC the previous year. He came back and vowed, as the legend goes, to go all out recruiting black athletes from the south. Once he "gave the word," all others followed suit. There had been an exception here and there prior to this, but this was a wholesale effort by the entire conference. It has been said because of this that he did more to integrate the South than a lot of others. Though this is not true, his actions were indeed significant.

Alabama would win the conference and finish 11-1. As a matter of record, here are the final standings after the bowl games, with records in parenthesis.

1 Nebraska (13-0)
2 Oklahoma (11-1)
3 Colorado (10-2) These three were all from the Big Eight Conference
4 Alabama (11-1)
5 Penn State (11-1)
6 Michigan (11-1)
7 Georgia (11-1)
8 Arizona St. (11-1)
9 Tennessee (10-2)

10 Stanford (9-3) Gave Michigan their only loss, in Rose
    Bowl
(In addition, L.S.U was 9-3 and Ole Miss and Auburn were
    10-2)

Alabama lost to Nebraska in the Orange Bowl and Auburn
    lost to Oklahoma in the Sugar Bowl.

This does not tell the entire story, however. Going into the
10th game of the year, Georgia hosted Auburn. On that Saturday,
Georgia, Alabama, and Auburn were all undefeated. Auburn,
ranked fifth, beat Georgia, ranked seventh, behind eventual
Heisman Trophy winner Pat Sullivan. Then the next week
Alabama, ranked third, beat Auburn. On that same weekend
Nebraska, ranked one, beat Oklahoma, ranked two, in a shootout
in what has been called the greatest game ever. This was all on
Thanksgiving Thursday. That night Georgia played Georgia Tech
in Atlanta. It was the first time the game happened on
Thanksgiving Day, and I was told later that it was also the first
time this game was a national broadcast.
    Georgia was flat, having lost the SEC championship the
previous game by virtue of losing to Auburn.
    Tech entered the game 6-4 behind the first black quarterback
in school history and one of the first anywhere in the south. They
had an uneven year as the record attests. They would lose their
bowl game to wind up 6-6, a record not indicative of their talent
level. They outplayed Georgia for 58 minutes and thirty-one
seconds.
    The last one minute and twenty-nine seconds will go down
as one of *the* best games in Ga. history. The last minute and a half
is all it took to make it a classic. I was there with a childhood
friend, and we got there already sated with the games from earlier
in the day. We sat in the Ga. section on the corner of the west
stands.
    Georgia got the ball on their own thirty-five-yard line, with
one minute and twenty-nine seconds left in regulation, needing a
touchdown to win, and they proceeded to drive to that touchdown
with fourteen seconds to spare. I later heard Larry Munson's call

of the drive, and it is a classic. That made the score 28-24 Georgia. They kicked back to Tech with a few seconds left.

That drive was a masterpiece by the sophomore quarterback from Athens, one of the greatest schoolboy athletes in Georgia history: Andy Johnson. He made several key completions to Lynn Hunicutt, an end against whom my friend and I had played in high school in Floyd County. Hunicutt was out of Pepperell High School in Lindale, Ga., and he ran ten and twelve yards at a time. Johnson made a 4th down completion to the tight end, and then Johnson ran for 22 yards to keep it going. Looking back, I don't see how they ran so many plays in such a short amount of time. Jimmy Poulos dove over the top of the defensive line to score!

Remember now, for most of this game we were sitting there—and I mean *sitting*, since there was not much to cheer about—contemplating how we would handle losing three in a row!

So much emotion had been pent up that when we scored, I left my seat, went down the aisle and onto the track and started running to my left towards the Tech alumni section in the east stands. Back then there were no impediments to doing so. Yelling and bragging, I almost got into several scrapes with Tech fans along the way. Because of that, and the fact that the game had just ended, I had to hurry back to my seat and find my friend!

This was the first Tech-Ga. game that occurred at night, was on artificial turf and was on national TV. It is this game that I sometimes refer to when asked where this series ranks among the other teams that Ga. plays. It will always be the most important. The feelings it engenders and the reactions it brings when the game unfolds as this did is unmatched. Winning when it looked like we had been beat, snatching victory from a certain third straight defeat, was exhilaration un-paralleled. It also convinced me that this type of victory is MUCH better than the type we enjoyed in, say, 1968. Vince Dooley rates it in his Top Ten.

I really could not sleep that night. It was late when we got back home to Rome, so I just kept replaying the victory in my head.

The game was a back and forth affair, but Ga. should have won going in anyway. They were ranked 7th going in, even after losing to Auburn. As I said, they were flat from losing the Auburn game. That would become a pattern. Whenever there was a lot on the line in the Auburn game and Ga. would lose, I would always fret that Tech may win, even when they were clearly not equal. Most of the time, Ga. would rally, sometimes late, to win. A few times they did not.

This Ga. team was one of the best in the university's history. They had four shutouts, and even though they lost by two touchdowns to Auburn, they were down one and driving late in the game. Sullivan to Beasley was just too much. They went on to beat North Carolina in the Gator Bowl, a team coached by Bill Dooley, Vince's brother and a former assistant coach under him at UGA. At the time, it was the only brother match-up in bowl history....It may still be.

The desultory ending to Tech's season, among other reasons, led to the firing of Bud Carson. He lasted five years following Bobby Dodd.

Ga. finished 11-1 and, as you saw, ranked 7th with that record. As I said, it was the greatest year in the history of college football.

1972

BACK IN ATHENS, this game was one of those that I have come to describe as uninspiringly played by two mediocre teams. Georgia's record was 7-4, with no subsequent bowl game, and Tech's was 7-4-1, which included an eventual bowl game that they won to get the 7th victory. Entering the game, Tech was 6-3-1 and Ga. was 6-4. At the end of the year Ga., as I said, had no bowl bid and was not ranked. Tech got a bowl, won it and finished ranked 20th. Why the consternation and repeated statement of facts? Georgia wins the 1972 game 27-7! Are you kidding me! Go figure.

Tech also had a new head coach, Bill Fulcher. He would only last two years, but I thought he fit the Tech mold and was a real class act.

The season had no particular highlights for either team, no upsets either way. The only thing that stood out is an incident in the Ga.-Ala. game, which I must relate. I was in the north stands on the isle between the sections where the two teams' seats meet. So there were a lot of Alabama fans around. Ga. lost by 20 or so, but late in the fourth quarter, Ga. was within the point spread and had the ball. If they scored, they would have cut the lead to less than one touchdown. (I cannot remember the exact spread, but trust me.) An Alabama fan stands up, waves a stack of bills, turns to the Ga. side and says, to the best of my recollection, "I have $200 here and I will bet anyone Alabama covers the points." Three or four Ga. fans stand up to try to take the bet. The Alabama man does, in fact, bet with one person. He sits down, and I am thinking, *Those folks are crazy, irrational and fools with their money…* when…BAM…Ga. fumbles, Alabama recovers and marches 40 yards or so to score with about a minute to go! From that point on, I really was afraid of Alabama and whatever mystic they had. A little scary. Bear does walk on water!

Back to Tech - Ga.

Andy Johnson and Jimmy Poulos were offensive stars for Ga., and the Bulldogs at that time were, well, shall we say, three yards and a cloud of dust would have been an understatement. I think that is why they received no bowl bid.

Somehow they put up 27 on Tech though, and it was a runaway from the start. About this time is when I started to think like a coach. All I could think of was all the reasons Ga. could lose and very few of why they could win. Especially in years when they came in with nearly identical records, it was hard to realistically think good thoughts. Only because it was a home game did it look somewhat promising.

I was in the corner of the north end zone near, what is now, the west stands. They were nonexistent then—only a scenic view of the railroad tracks.

Tech played uninspired, and I think that was the knock on Fulcher. This victory gave Ga. two in a row again after those two straight losses a few years earlier. Fans were quieted, but you could tell there was an undercurrent. I really think the disappointment of the '71 season had a season-long hangover in '72.

1973

IT WAS YET ANOTHER LACKLUSTER year for Tech and Ga. For Ga., it would prove to be a very confusing year that gave rise to a lot of discontent by fans, which I think spilled over into 1974 and is why that team was very bad. More on them later.

This was Johnson's and Poulos's and other stars' last year—some of those sophomore stars from that 1971 team.

Here is what they did during the year. Hold on as you will get dizzy.

Ga. finished with a 7-4-1 record with a victory over Maryland in the Peach Bowl at Atlanta-Fulton Co. Stadium. I was at that game also, and it was fun. It was here "in town" at the baseball park, but to me it was a bowl game—my first—and I loved it.

They started the season with a tie, 7 to 7, against Pittsburg and a freshman, 150-pound running back named Tony Dorsett. In a freak of irony, he would play his last game against Ga. also in the 1977 Sugar Bowl for the national championship. More on that later.

They lost to Alabama, again, over there in one of the biggest, most blatantly crooked calls in their history. Georgia was driving for the tying touchdown, and the ref literally took the ball away from the offense and Alabama went on to score one more time. That's all I can say about that...other than this. It killed their spirit. They beat Ole Miss but lost to both Kentucky and Vanderbilt. Then they had a gift given to them by UT. The famous "4th and dumb" play in Knoxville, where Tennessee went for it (by faking a punt) on their own, I think, 30-yard line, and Ga. held. Ga went on to win, and this is one of the ten highlight calls by Larry Munson, in my opinion. Then they lost to Florida by one and beat Auburn.

Tech, meanwhile, played a soft schedule and still went into this game 5-5. That would prove to be the end of the Fulcher Era, all two years of it. Guess it was not what Tech wanted after all. They are so impatient sometimes.

They beat nobody of consequence, and that is why, even though Ga. won, it was discouraging. The score was 10-3, and we had to have a goal line stand to win. A freshman linebacker, Sylvester Boler, made the tackle. It was the first time I felt that way in a victory. I was now out of college and had a little more perspective—a little, not a lot—but I left Grant Field feeling empty. We won, yes, but not in a way that made you proud. Deep down you know a better Tech team could have won. Bear in mind, the talent level was still wide apart in Georgia's favor and Ga. simply should have won big, even in Atlanta. But, yes, we were still satisfied that Ga. won and it goes in the record as such.

The only good thing was that this was the second time I went with my Dad. We actually sat in the old horseshoe end zone, like we did in 1969. 'Nuff said about that game, much like 1972. It was getting to be a boring habit. But like the year before, I was nervous because I did not know which "team" would show up— the one that lost to Vandy or the one that played Alabama toe to toe.

Again, there was no offense and the marginal fans were howling for Vince's scalp. He himself admits that this was the toughest time in his tenure.

1974

Gather 'round people and you shall hear
Of the worst Tech-Georgia game of any year.
I say this as a Ga. fan,
Tech fans would disagree,
But listen closely and you will see,
It never will be worse than the year after 1973.
Friday was a spring-like day,
We all arrived dressed that way.
Saturday dawned and we looked at Athens town
What had happened, there was sleet falling down!
Oh well, we went to the game,
Pepper's first year, we would have him tamed.
Tech was 5-5 entering the game,
Ga. was 6-4, very much the same.
For the third straight year they both were bland,
But, heck, this was Tech, so strike up the band!
A victory here and all would be well,
What happened was it went all to hell!
Tech won, 34-14, the worst ever under Vince,
Those that wanted him gone,
Saw this as the clinch.
The wishbone was crushing, we were all in a snit!
The snow and ice made it worse,
We could not stop it.
By the half it was over, we Bulldogs knew that,
We were freezing, why wasn't Tech?!
For the only time ever,
I left before it was over.
I was in a short sleeve shirt, what was Georgia's excuse?

No one on our side had any type of cover.
Munson said when the game was near complete,
There was nothing but Tech fans…
Sanford had yellow in every seat.
No Bulldog fans in sight,
What a dreadful sight.
Oh, what a dreadful sight.
But every cloud has a silver lining,
This game led to a 1975 Bulldog shining!

Truly this game is etched in the minds of all Tech and Georgia fans, for totally different reasons. Even though we knew Ga. had underperformed and there was a LOT of heat to "Dump Dooley," most of us felt Ga. would still win because Tech was not good either. But I have to hand it to Pepper Rodgers. He had them ready and running that wishbone like Alabama or Oklahoma. Our defense that year was probably one of, if not the, worst ever under Erk Russell. A bad combination to be sure. The game conditions cannot be described. It is to this day the only Tech-Ga. game played in freezing ice or snow during this stretch. The Tech fans had driven over that morning, so they dressed accordingly. Those of us who came to Athens the night before did not. It was miserable because of the weather, in addition to the play. We were under the upper deck in the north stands—no coats, no hats, not even long sleeve shirts. The group of us left at halftime and went and sat in our cars to listen to the rest of the game. I have never been more miserable at any game, and it had to be against Ga. Tech!

Tech finished 6-5 and did not go to a bowl. And boy, did they brag about that game—for the entire year. But only for a year; more on that in a minute.

Ga. lost four of their last five games, beating only Florida; they were several close losses but losses nonetheless. The last loss, to Miami of Ohio in the Tangerine Bowl, was about as humiliating a loss as I have ever seen suffered by Ga.

Even counting '69 and '70 with break-even seasons and two straight losses to Tech, this was the lowest ebb of Ga. football under Vince. After ten years he was in a "do or die" situation.

1975

HE WOULD "DO." Thankfully, though they did not develop quickly enough to avert the results incurred in 1974, there was a good core of players that would provide two great years and save Vince's job. The '75 Tech game ranks as one of the best ever for a number of reasons. To get right to the point, Ga. won 42-26. This team, led by Ray Goff, Matt Robinson, Glynn Harrison, Gene Washington, Richard Appleby, Joe Tereshinski, Steve and Mike Wilson, as well as Ben Zambiasi, Bill Krug, Johnny Henderson and others did something few teams have done, even when they won the SEC. They beat Florida, Auburn and Tech. They lost to Arkansas in the Cotton Bowl, finishing 10-2, and 5-1 in the conference.

They lost in the regular season to Pittsburg and Tony Dorsett again and to Ole Miss.

Of course, this is the year of the Florida "Appleby to Washington" game and the immortal call of Larry Munson.

Tech was 7-4 but did not go to a bowl. You could say they were lackluster because they only beat mediocre teams and lost to all the good ones they played…UGA, Notre Dame, Auburn and so forth. But they were feeling their oats as we came to Atlanta. As I have mentioned, I was worried about this game for one reason…that daggum wishbone and wondering how would we stop it. They were still talking about the '74 game and how Ga. would never win again. Heck, even some Ga. "fans" were saying that.

It was freezing cold, but compared to the previous year, it felt great. Cold, clear, no wind and on Thanksgiving night, again, on TV. We sat in the old horseshoe end zone of the south stands. It was not a good vantage point, but we did get to see Glidin'

Glynn Harrison's butt flying down the field a few times on long runs.

I gave the score, but it was much worse than that. It was 42-0 before Tech scored. Pepper would say after the game, and I guess this is all he had to hang his hat on, "Well, we are still ahead in total points, by four."

It was a classic example of how big of a part motivation can play in sports, especially football and basketball. We were very concerned going in because, even with the great accomplishments of this team, we still had to face that dreaded wishbone. It was, in several ways, much more intimidating than the offense of Paul Johnson.

Georgia remembered 1974, but more than that they remembered the mouthing off by Tech in the ensuing twelve months. I know Ga. fans mouth off a lot, but they have some reason for doing so. Going into the 1974 game, Dooley was 8-2. Tech wins one time—impressively yes—but you would have thought they had run off a winning streak. It was one game, and a very good one for them, but you have to follow that up. They did not.

Ga. let up in the second half, and I was upset they did so, but the game is still one of the very best ever. Revenge is ever so sweet.

This team finished up beating Florida, Auburn and Tech, something that, up to that point, only teams that won championships had done. So, at the end of the game Vince said they, too, were champions.

1976

THIS IS ONE OF THE BEST TEAMS in UGA history: SEC champions, 21-0 victors over Bear and Alabama. Yes, it was a shutout of Alabama, which was extremely rare. There was only one regular season loss, yet again to Ole Miss by 4 points over there, the week after defeating Alabama. Final regular season ranking—5— going into the Sugar Bowl against #1 ranked Pittsburg, yes, with Tony Dorsett.

This team had it all. Ray Goff, a running quarterback, who became player of the year in the conference; Matt Robinson, the throwing quarterback, who would go on to a long pro career; Kevin McLee, a punishing runner, one of Georgia's best ever; and a punishing defense (see Alabama!). Besides shutting out Alabama, they also shut out Clemson, Auburn and one more, for a total of four. We even had a great kicker, Alan Leavitt—the first of an incredibly long string of excellent kickers that continues to this day. This is the team that beat Florida in one of the best Ga.-Fla. games ever. They were down 27-13 at halftime and came back and outscored Florida 28-0 in the second half—all on the ground, with Goff scoring five touchdowns!

Tech, on the other hand, entered the game 4-5-1. They beat a 9-3 Notre Dame team but lost the next week to Navy. Another Pepper team that seemed to always underperform.

Ga. won 13-10. You would have thought with what you just read about the respective seasons that it would have been like 1968. But it was not. It was pretty cold and considerably overcast, with sprinkles throughout. The field became muddy and Ga. sleep-walked through it until the very end.

We were driving for a touchdown but fumbled. Tech then had the ball with only a few minutes left and the score tied. Then they fumbled! Unbelievable! We ran a couple of plays and lined up for a relatively short field goal. In these conditions, it was not a given, even with Leavitt. Well, he made the kick. He was fairly small, and he ran over to the Tech side (the attempt was on their end and on the right hash mark) and shook his fists at them for a long time! I was sitting at that end in the north stands down low and could get a good look at it. What a sight. I felt like he felt. Then, going home, I felt bad because the game was not a good one for Ga. We were lucky to win, to be honest. Except for the 1975 game, Tech played Ga. tough and Pepper, believe it or not, had one of the best percentages against Ga. during this 50 year period.

Post-Script: we were demolished in the Sugar Bowl. I never asked Ray Goff why; I thought it was none of my business and best to keep in the past. If Ga. had won, they could have been in serious contention for the mythical national championship, which is all that existed then.

1977

NOT A GOOD YEAR OVERALL, in the Tech game and for the team. They had a lot of problems. Just when it appeared Vince had things straightened out and headed up again, this year comes along. They enter the game 5-5, lose, and finish with the first, and only, losing season under Vince Dooley.

They started out beating Oregon and losing to Clemson 7-6. Then they won a couple, went to Tuscaloosa and played the eventual #2 team in the country but lost 18-10. It was close. I was at that game—the only one I have ever seen on campus there. We looked good at times and then other times not, indicative of the entire year. That defeat broke their spirit and they lost their last three, including 33-0 to Kentucky. Kentucky had a really good team, their best since Bear coached there. The highlight of the game was that Prince Charles was in attendance. This is the team that was later "busted" by the NCAA, and everything they earned was vacated, including their SEC crown.

One very unusual note on this season: only three SEC teams had winning records!

Tech also entered this game 5-5. They had done better throughout the year than Ga., winning a couple of games against teams Ga. had lost to. But, guess what? I felt we would win, even with it being in Atlanta. Usually when both teams are not good (otherwise known as bad) Ga. won most of the time. Not this year.

It was a very cold, clear day and we were in the same section that Tech allots to most Ga. fans, the corner of the east stands next to the old horseshoe.

Ga. played the—I kid you not—sixth-string quarterback (due to injuries) and still only lost 16-7. The game had no real highlights, no great plays and, in spite of the score, was not a nail-biter. It was just a bad game, but it was a Tech-Ga. game nonetheless. There was intensity and interest, but nobody other than true fans of both teams cared! I remember walking away on the track from our seats and looking at the play of the final few seconds, thinking, *How could we have gotten so bad to lose to this bad team?*

It was a bad year and guess what? Pepper was 2-2 against Ga. Not good. Now he was "ahead" by 10 points in the 4 games, according to his process of success.

1978

AS HAD BECOME A HABIT under Vince, a bad year was followed by a good year. This was 1978, the year of the Wonder Dogs!

This is also the year that had one of the top five or six best games ever in the series, 29-28 DAWGS. Vince himself said a few years back that it was *the* most exciting game he ever saw! It had everything: punt returns, kickoff returns, onside kicks, interceptions, going for two.

This Ga. team did a lot of remarkable things and had a number of interesting facts surrounding the year.

They would finish 9-2-1, with one of those losses coming in the Bluebonnet Bowl against Stanford. Their quarterback was Steve Dils and their head coach was Bill Walsh. The other loss came against South Carolina in the second game. They won every other game as the year rolled along until they went to Auburn. This is the year Rex Robinson hit a long, late field goal against Kentucky that gave rise to another classic Munson call. This is the year we went to LSU and were getting beat, when a freshman ran back the opening second half kickoff for a touchdown and Ga. sailed from there. His name is Lindsey Scott. I was at that game, my first ever there, and it was truly unique. It is really a special place.

I drive over to Auburn for the anticipated win there to capture the SEC, but it didn't happen. We did not lose either. This was a 22-22 tie. It was one of the most hard-fought, intense, back-and-forth games I have ever seen. We were lucky to tie, to be honest. We could have gone for two after scoring with about five minutes left in the game, but Vince opted to play defense and try for a field goal. That was the mindset back then by a lot of coaches. Auburn had three running backs that would go on to have professional careers, and they weren't just on a roster—they had good careers. They were William Andrews, Joe Cribbs and James Brooks. Auburn had a so-so year, but that day they were outstanding. Attribute it to the nature of the Ga.-Auburn series.

As was the case so many times, coming that close to winning the SEC and still coming up short left Ga. in a funk. That funk typically carries over to the Tech game, even with a week off most of the time.

Tech had their best team by far under Pepper. They had Eddie Lee Ivory, who amassed 1,562 yards rushing, an astounding total back then. They lost their first two but then reeled off seven wins in a row. Then they lost to Notre Dame and that led them into Athens for the last game.

Hang on, as this is one of the best games ever.

The day started out cloudy and we were sitting in the corner on the lower deck of the south stands just near the wall, about near the top of the lower section. We could see and feel the fans on the bridge. Two feet more to the right, and we would have been on "the bank"—a grassy area that does not exist now.

Tech jumped out to a 20-0 lead, two touchdowns and two field goals. I was devastated and really thought that it was over. This is one of those games I worried about going into it, and those worries were confirmed...until late in the second quarter. It was the first Tech game that my oldest son went to, but that did not keep me from being in a bad mood. My youngest had just been born in August.

Sometime in the second quarter, Vince brings in the freshman quarterback, Buck Belue. He would play virtually the rest of the game. Late in the second quarter, Willie McClendon, player of the year in the SEC, scores to make it 20-7, Tech. At that moment, I swear, the sun came out. All of a sudden I had hope—we had new life, and we would start the second half with the ball.

We score at the start of the second half and cut the lead to 20-14. McClendon again—not a bad back himself, with 1,312 yards rushing. He was the father of Coach Bryan McClendon.

Then the fireworks really started.

After several swaps of possession, Tech punted. Scott Woerner returned it for a touchdown. He broke, I think, six tackles, meanwhile Munson is screaming, "Woerner, Woerner, Woerner!" We now have the lead 21-20. On the ensuing kickoff, their speedster, Drew Hill returns the kickoff 101 yards for a touchdown. Now we are down. They go for two and make it, so we are down 28-21. In less than two minutes, 15 points were scored, and the lead changed twice!

We were now in the last five minutes and were 85 yards away from the goal. Belue engineered—no pun intended—one of the greatest drives in Bulldog history. They went for it twice on fourth down. On the second one, at Tech's 46, with two yards needed, he scrambled, found Amp Arnold in the clear and heaved it to him for a score. Sound somewhat familiar?

Now we were going for two. On the first one, we threw and they pass interfered. We tried again. Reverse option, our fullback goes the wrong way, and Belue was pressured but managed to pitch to Arnold, who pranced into the end zone for a 29-28 lead.

There was still time so Tech got it and was driving down to, I believe, Georgia's 35. They threw and it was intercepted by, I think, Scott Woerner (I know he had one in the game). That's it...Ga. wins a thriller. Enough? Buck Belue has said it is his favorite game—not '80 Florida, not the Sugar Bowl, but this one.

For a long time this would be recounted as the greatest Tech-Ga. game ever. We will discuss later if it still is considered so.

This was one of those games where I was now in the camp of "the best games are the exciting ones and if, by chance, we come from behind and break their heart, all the better." The feeling you have is that you can conquer all your own problems...being in a good mood is an understatement!

1979

THIS WAS POSSIBLY the weirdest season in Georgia annals. They enter the Tech game 5-5. They lost all four non-conference games. They won all five conference games up to the Auburn game. That included a win over #13 LSU. If Ga. beat Auburn, and the game was played in Athens, they would be conference champs with, at that point, a 6-4 record.

It was not to be. Belue breaks his ankle and Ga. loses.

So, as I have mentioned before, they travel to Atlanta to play Tech after a devastating loss to Auburn.

Tech is not very good either. It would be Pepper's last game. He sensed that and "campaigned" to be retained, but it was not to be. They would finish 4-6-1, and the tie was with Florida! They came into the Ga. game on a three-game winning streak over Duke, Air Force and Navy, to be 4-5-1. Well....that is a winning streak. They needed to beat Ga. to avoid a losing season.

Georgia needed a win to have a winning season and, more importantly, to avoid another losing one, which would have been the second in three years. Ga. has to play their third-string quarterback, so naturally I am nervous coming in. We sit in the same Ga. section in the east stands, and it is another sunny day—sunny but *really* cold. It was probably colder than the '75 night game, but with the sun it felt a little better.

Ga. wins 16-3, but it is really closer than that. For a long time Tech was within a score to tie or lead, so it was a tense game—a poorly played game, but tense nonetheless. Jeff Pyburn was quarterback, and it was his last game for Ga. There's not much to give as far as highlights. Sound familiar? This is getting to be redundant—1974, 1977, 1979. It was a depth in the series, with desultory results from both sides, at the same time, that had not been reached maybe ever before.

I remember feeling nothing after the game. It was the first time I had experienced that. It was as if the luster had come off the series. What it was, though, was the realization for me that Georgia's program was at a crossroads and it was not much further ahead than where Tech's program was. Depressing!

Pepper would finish, believe it or not, with one of the better records against Ga., other than Bobby Dodd. He was 2-4, and that includes the thriller in 1978 and 1976. He could easily have been 4-2.

1980, 1981, 1982

I THOUGHT OF HOW to present these years, under Herschel and others, without being redundant, so I decided to present them as a package. They are all very similar and have similar results. Specifically, I'll cover the seasons generally as a whole, the Tech games specifically, and the standings of the Dawgs nationally. No need to go over these three seasons in detail, however; they have been detailed enough. Suffice to say, the winning streak by Georgia continued during the Walker years and a little beyond.

The three scores were, respectively, 38-20, 44-7 and 38-18, all Georgia victories. Herschel ran for 205, 225 and 162 yards in those three years. That's a total of 592 yards. Incredible! Georgia's records were 12-0, 10-2 and 11-1. Two of those three defeats were in bowls. So there was only *one* defeat in three regular seasons! That's an unbelievable run of success. Tech, meanwhile, was 1-9-1, 1-10 and 6-5.

Now here's a little on each game.

By the time Tech came to Athens in 1980, the die was cast. Even I was not concerned about the outcome. Munson was, maybe, but not many of the rest of us were. The score is not indicative of the way Georgia dominated. There is a legendary picture of one of Tech's defensive backs chasing Herschel on a long TD run. I found out from this game that when the outcome is so expected and then actually happens, it renders the game less exciting than normal. I will say, I was not happy that Tech scored twenty points! That was way too many for the level of talent comparison. The game was gratifying, don't misunderstand me, but there is an absence of that edge. You find out you miss that edge. You start to wonder if you want it the other way. After all, sports competition is all about adrenaline and excitement. When there is no suspense, is it as fulfilling? Georgia enters the game #1 in the country, and believe it or not, it was all thanks to Tech tying Notre Dame a few weeks earlier. Georgia was coming off a thrilling victory over Auburn, in Auburn, that clinched the conference. I cannot remember if, at this point, the bowls had been set; if so, it was known Ga. would be playing Notre Dame.

We sat down low in the corner of the end zone next to the Ga. Redcoat band. They were not good seats, but I was there!

In 1981, we are in Grant Field, at the normal site where we sit—lower corner, East stands, with other Dawg fans. The mood is very much the same as the year before. Only the weather is better—sunny, chilly, but pleasant. Tech is no better than the year before and Georgia, in mine and many others' opinion, has a better team than the national championship edition.

On the first play, Belue fades back after a fake to Herschel, who dives into the pile of Tech defenders thinking he would run, and lofts a bomb to Lindsey Scott, who goes in for a long TD. As the headline in the Atlanta newspaper said the next morning, "BOOM, one play, call it a day!"

It was a great call and a great headline. I used to keep each headline when Georgia won, and put it up on my desk where I worked for the coming year. That about sums it up.

The only suspense is to see how many penalties Tech gets for unnecessary roughness or unsportsmanlike conduct. Again, there were the same feelings and the same lack of fulfillment, but it was a satisfying victory and a winning streak reaching four now.

In 1982 the game is back in Athens, and there is some pre-game chatter that it might be competitive this year. Tech has a winning record, but Georgia is undefeated and ranked number one...again! To me, there is no doubt who will win. Who cares if it is closer—not close, but *relatively* closer? It winds up actually being a little bigger of a victory for Ga., point differential-wise, than in 1980.

This is my assumption: playing this game seemed like a necessary detail Georgia had to get done before going to the Sugar Bowl to win the national championship. Here's what I mean: by this time, after three incredible years of domination—

not just of Tech, but the entire schedule—one gets a sense of inevitability at games. There is no suspense, no drama, no expectation that a loss is even possible. I remember thinking, *This is what Alabama fans felt like in the seventies.* That is not good. I realize that while this is a situation that most coaches and programs do not experience but think they would love to, it actually creates an entirely new set of problems. If the coaches are not aware and prepared for it, it can lead to a drop in results. To the Ga. coaching staff's credit, that did not occur, at least for several more years. It is part and parcel, I think, of why Vince started casting his eye towards politics. Human nature is such that once you reach your goals, year after year, it is extremely hard to be motivated to continue. That is why coaches say it is harder to stay on top than get on top.

This feeling I have been describing grows out of this situation. The ultimate danger is this: fans get to a point where they think it is supposed to happen, going to happen and when it does not, all of a sudden, they are disappointed and think the program is "going down." I will, however, say that it was fun (in a "top dog" kind of way) to experience it once just to know that feeling and to have it eventually make you appreciate the good years much more than ever before.

Ga. wins their fifth in a row, and that does feel good, regardless of how easy it was.

1983

THIS WAS A VERY INTERESTING year, a year that I think is underappreciated and unacknowledged as having one of Georgia's best teams ever. Led by All-Americans Kevin Butler and Terry Hogue, Ga. only lost once, with one tie in the regular season to Clemson, up there. The loss was to #3 Auburn by 7, in Athens. At the time, Ga. was ranked fourth. It was a classic game where sophomore Bo Jackson had his coming out, as far as I was concerned. I was at that game and remember thinking, *We cannot be getting beat. Who is this guy?*

Georgia beat UCLA, ranked 20th, to open the season. It rained during the game, and my two sons and I had to go under the stands to try to stay dry. At night, it was a great game. They beat #9 Florida by one point, and in a thriller—yes, a thriller—beat Vandy by one touchdown. This is the game, highlighted by another Munson classic, where Terry Hogue proved his Heisman credentials. He finished 5th in the voting that year.

Tech, on the other hand, had digressed. They went 3-8. This was their first year in the ACC and it did not go well.

So we head to Grant Field and sit in the upper deck in the south section, near the end zone at the west end. It was sunny, cool, and my youngest son's first game. (More on that later.).

We are good, Tech is bad, and yet the game is a struggle. We do not play well—uninspired. Why? Remember, Ga. had lost the SEC championship to Auburn in the previous game. This is a recurring theme that is hard to shake and has enough history to tell you beforehand what to expect. So, going in, I am worried, despite the records.

Ga. wins 27-24 and only a late interception by the Dawgs saves them. This is the first game (not even in 1976 did I feel this) where Georgia was clearly better and won, yet I came away disgusted and concerned. Again, we had become so used to winning that when it was not a blowout against a bad team, you would have thought we lost. But I think I was correct in being concerned. It appeared to me, even with a bad Tech team, that they were closing the gap and were starting to believe they could beat Georgia. That is most of the battle—believing. Before now, they really did not believe, or so it appeared. Now I thought they did.

Ga. goes on and wins the Cotton Bowl against Texas 10-9 in one of the greatest games ever and one of the biggest upsets ever. The season wound up 10-1-1 for Georgia, and they were ranked 4th at the end of the year. But that Tech game was still gnawing at me. For good reason; there is always next year to worry about.

1984

THE GNAWING GROWS into full-on devouring.

Ga. enters the game 7-3. Tech enters 5-4-1. Ga. beat Alabama, in Alabama, who was #2 at the time. Then they beat Clemson, then lost to S. Carolina, then won 5 in a row and rose to 8th in the country. Then they lost to Florida badly and to Auburn. Tech also beats Alabama and Clemson the week after Ga. beat them but lost or tied their next four games. They would finish third in the conference.

All indicators would seem to point to a Georgia victory in Athens. What do I mean?

I have written about culture and history. That was weighing heavily in Georgia's favor in 1984. Consider this: we had just won three conference championships and lost a fourth by a touchdown to Auburn, to start the decade. Then factor in Herschel and his winning the Heisman, and Terry Hogue coming in 5th a year later. Our women's basketball team was becoming a national powerhouse. Our men's basketball team had had three years of Dominique and then a trip to the final four. The mindset in Dawg Land was, "How could we lose?" We had done so little of it for half a decade.

But I was still remembering the 1983 game, and by the time I was in my seat at Sanford Stadium, I could see a different attitude in the Tech players. Well-observed. Tech would win 35-18. It was an upset of gigantic proportions if you watched the game and think about the score.

Ga. was never in it, and Tech poured it on. I was with my sons and we were in the lower stands on the south side right next to the Tech contingent. It was a tough game to watch and stay for. Georgia clearly was not inspired, like they did not care. It reminded me of 1973 and 1974. That is what gnaws at you the most. How could they not care? Of course, this is one of those times where the chatter starts about this not being a "real" rivalry. I really believe the players buy into that. They certainly played like it did not matter. Tech played like their lives depended on it.

John Dewberry, a Ga. transfer, played the game of his career and then proceeded to rip off some of the hedges and chew on them. The gnawing continued. I had flashbacks to the 1974 ice game of ten years ago, to the day.

Reflecting on this game in the days after it was over, I developed a better appreciation of winning, even when it was expected and easy. This game put a whole new perspective on things. One I have not forgotten to this day. I cherish every victory—no matter how easy or anticipated, no matter how hard or difficult, no matter how it is achieved…well-played or not. I try to explain that to others who have not experienced enough types of games to understand this. But watch enough, and you will see and agree.

1985

ANOTHER DEFEAT, this time in Atlanta, at night in the fog, and the three of us (my sons and I) were sitting in the upper deck, east side.

Going into this game I had mixed feelings. Ga. was 7-2-1 going in and Tech was 7-2-1. We had recent history to factor in, it was in Atlanta, and it was Curry's best team to date. But just how good were they? They had not beaten anybody of consequence. They did tie Tennessee in Knoxville. With an ultimate record of 9-2-1, they were only ranked 19th at the end of the season. Plus, Ga. had had an up-and-down year but had beaten #1 Florida in a classic game of that series. The team had rushed for almost 300 yards, led by Lars Tate, Tim Worley, and Keith Henderson. It was the best running backfield in America, especially when you factor in the quarterback's total of almost 400.

Georgia had lost a heartbreaker to Alabama at home in the opening game, which we went to. Then we went to the Tech game, bookends. Georgia's quarterback, James Jackson was one of those whom you held your breath with. One play he was superman and the next he was Willie Coyote, a disaster waiting to happen.

As I said, it was a foggy night, unseasonably warm, and we were in the upper deck. On top of that, low clouds rolled in. And on top of that, some kind of gun or cannon was fired, and if you've seen it before, you know that the smoke from it settles over the field. This was on TV, and I wish I could have had one in front of me at that moment. We saw literally almost nothing until well into the second half!

It was an exciting game, with both teams holding leads back and forth. The second half was just as good. Ga. came up short trying to score on a last drive that would have won the game. They lost 20-16.

I really was concerned we would lose as we drove to Grant Field, but as the game went along, I felt better and better. It was a very frustrating game with all the mistakes we made. Tech (I am not going to say this many times) was probably a better team, but we had every chance to win.

Now Ga. had lost two in a row for the first time since '69 and '70…fifteen years. This happened after winning six in a row. Curry was now 2-4 against Georgia. I mention that because this was when he started taking off after Vince and UGA. If you want to know more, you can read up on it. It is one of— if not the— main reason I have no use for Bill Curry. If he had kept his mouth shut, there is no telling what would have happened in the series. As it was, he only served to rekindle the competitive spirit in Vince and the entire Bulldog community, after they had admittedly gone through a period of complacency. Thanks, Bill! "Shining" knights on white horses usually fall off!

1986

AS I MENTIONED, after the past two years (down years for Ga. compared to the start of the decade), Ga. improves in all facets. Of course, most teams would be experiencing a drop-off from those first four years and still have a good team. The fact is, however, all Ga. had to do during the post-Herschel years was beat who they should beat, plus beat Tech. Instead, they lost to Tech, and that one game made a world of difference. Winning would have put a salve on a lot of feelings and improved the records just enough for it to be viewed as a great season.

So we go to Athens with Ga. sporting a 7-3 record and Tech with 5-4-1. Tech had slid from the "height" they had reached and Ga., despite the three losses, had made strides. We lost a close one to LSU down there; a bunch of us had gone down hoping for a repeat of 1978. This is also the year of the famous "hose game" at Auburn. Ga. wins that game 31-24.

Curry always managed to get his guys sky high, more than some others at Tech did, and if he had any talent, they would keep it close.

Georgia went on and lost their bowl game to finish 8-4, which at that point was not great but would serve as a transition team and transition year for the next two.

The game itself was what I would call engaging. Close, with a lot of lead changes and the outcome up in the air; but it was not very well played. So, to me, it was not exciting, but it was satisfying. The final score was 31-24. This was one of the few times that I think the rousing victory over Auburn actually served to make Georgia view this game as an afterthought. They knew nothing could top the Auburn victory, especially over a .500 football team, even if it was Tech.

This would turn out to be Curry's last year. He leaves for Alabama. We all felt part of his reason for leaving his alma mater was he knew the cupboard of talent, while it had ascended to a point, was quickly being depleted. He could not recruit on a consistent basis. Now, why Alabama hired him is another question, one for others to answer.

1987

So Bobby Ross comes in with what he has to work with and goes 2-9, not beating any Division I school. It was an absolute disaster and one which he crawled out from. In my opinion, he is the best coach Tech has had since Bobby Dodd. See 1990.

Georgia, meanwhile, enters the Tech game in Atlanta "only" 7-3. They have a tough loss to LSU at home, one to Auburn in Athens, and the other to Clemson, there, by one point on a very controversial play.

They are better than their record indicates, and that is why they are ranked. Ga. wins fairly easily 30-16 and we are again in the east upper deck. Once again, the weather is bad, but not the same as in 1985. We actually see the game below. This is a better game—better played—and like the year before, I am worried going in. But really, in the back of my mind, I feel there is very little chance of Tech winning. This Georgia team rushes for over 300 yards, led by Lars Tate and a freshman, Rodney Hampton. By now, James Jackson has matured greatly as a player and quarterback. Great players on defense, Bill Goldberg, Ben Smith, Will Jones and others, made this a team with great potential. They just came up short during the year and, I think, took it out on Tech and Arkansas in the bowl, which they won. So, after it is all over, they have a 9-3 record, the best record since the '83 team.

1988

THE IMPROVEMENT CARRIES over into the next year. Although the records are identical when Ga. enters the Tech game as they were in 1987, they just played better...with two exceptions. They lost to Kentucky, which cost them the conference championship. They lost to Auburn, who did win it and was ranked 9th at the time. Then they lost to South Carolina, by a lot. Unexplainable. Later—get this—Tech beats South Carolina by a lot and shuts them out, when the Gamecocks were ranked 8th. What else did Tech do? Beat two non-Division I teams. Yes, in two years they had exactly one victory against Division I teams, and it was against a team that beat Ga. So Tech comes to Athens with a 3-7 record against Georgia's 7-3. I was still concerned because of that Gamecock game (always something you can point at to show why you should be concerned, even when rational thought demands otherwise).

This is Vince's last year, last game against Tech, and last home game ever. When I sat in the stands with my sons, I was more scared that Ga. would lose *his* last game then I was that they would lose to Tech. I wanted a win for a great coach. Twenty-five years have flown by, in many ways. We are in the upper deck again on the south side, as before, and as the game progressed, it was obvious that Ga. would win. I remember thinking, at that point in time, *Remember, this Ross guy is going to be a piece of cake*...The only question is, would he last long enough? We would get our answer way too quickly.

Led by Tim Worley, Keith Henderson, and Rodney Hampton, Ga. literally ran all over Tech. The final score was 24-3. Wayne Johnson, who had a strong and accurate arm, was basically just a player to hand the ball off—a fate many quarterbacks at Ga. have had.

I remember the end of the game when Ross gave a cursory congrats to Vince as the Georgia players carried him off on their shoulders. I found myself overwhelmed with emotion. I remembered back to 1966, to the 1965 Alabama game, and all the many memories and realized that, heck, I was getting older also. My sons asked if I was alright. I said yes…But I was thinking that this was the only coach I had really known so far and the only coach my sons knew. I would miss him.

1989

THE NEW GA. COACH is Ray Goff, and he inherits a pretty good stable of talent, led by Rodney Hampton. We had minimal effectiveness at quarterback, and some of that was due to the strong running game. We did have a good defense. Ga. was 6-3 heading into the Auburn game. Earlier they had lost by a total of 7 points to Tennessee and Ole Miss at their places. They did beat Florida and Emmitt Smith. But they lost to Auburn, Tech, and Syracuse, by one point, in the Peach Bowl.

Tech, on the other hand, was 6-4 coming into Ga. game. They lost their first three and went 7-1 the rest of their schedule, including a victory over Georgia. Shawn Jones was the quarterback, and if you were paying attention, you could see that all of a sudden everything clicked with Ross' way and Tech became the team that would, the next year, win every game but one and be national champions, at least according to UPI and the coaches.

I am sure you can guess my next statement. In spite of all the evidence, I felt UGA would win. I was nervous going in, yes, but I still believed that the Tech season had been smoke and mirrors, and we were 7 points away from being 8-2.

The fact is, we were winning as the first half was winding down. Then, BAM! Hampton hurt his knee and was finished for the game…and his career at UGA, for that matter. Ga. was finished, too. The entire second half belonged to Tech and they won going away, 22-33.

I was with my youngest son in the box at Tech, courtesy of friends I had there. Yes, I did have, and still do have, Tech friends.

It was overcast, and when Hampton goes down, our mood becomes overcast also. I kind of felt like that was the game. I was not giving up but was just realizing that he was all we had, and without him, we had no offense. I also remember later the next week or so that Tech was a *lot* better than they had been previously. I wondered what Ross had done, how he had done it and just how high their ceiling was. I immediately started worrying about the game the next year. This team, Tech, did not look like any Tech team I had seen since the '70 edition. It would get worse for us.

1990

TO BE CHARITABLE, you could say this was a transition year. We still had no powerful quarterback, but we did have a freshman running back, Garrison Hearst. We had some good players on defense but not enough. We started the season losing at LSU by only five then beat Alabama at home. Then near the end, the season collapses with us losing to Kentucky, Florida, Auburn, and Tech. None of the games were close but Kentucky, where Georgia comes within two points of winning.

Tech has a season for the ages. Tying only North Carolina, they win the ACC and beat Ga. 40-23. Then they beat Nebraska in the Orange Bowl for a part of a national title. They win the UPI and come in second in the AP polls. These are how the champions were crowned back then, purely arbitrary and never with head-to-head match-ups.

They were very balanced—no great stars at any position but a lot of very steady, good players. They ran for over 2,000 yards and passed for over 2,000.

Going over to Athens with my sons, I was contemplative (remember, UGA is 4-6 entering this game) about whether or not it was even a possibility that the Bulldogs could win. I rationalized a number of scenarios but knew that they all were unlikely, except one: we play our best game and they play their worst. It could happen.

I had a sideline pass, and my sons sat in our ticketed seats in the stands. I heard on the sideline that Herschel had spoken to them in the locker room the day before. That gave me hope. I know it makes no sense, but that is how a fanatic for sports thinks, or rather, does *not* think!

It is close for a little over a quarter, and UGA actually scores first on a Hearst run. That kind of occurrence makes you think, *I believe it could happen.* Then Tech opens a decent lead—not insurmountable, but more than a touchdown. When the second half starts, I have a glimmer of hope. That is dashed quickly as Ga. makes mistakes and Tech does not. By the fourth quarter, it is hopeless. Remember, Tech is the eventual national champion, and UGA winds up 4-7. Getting beat by 17 is not really an embarrassment considering the vast difference in success between the two teams.

For some reason this feeling was not nearly as bad as in 1974. Tech was really good and we were really *not* good. It was the single most definite example of Tech being clearly better. They should have won and they did, resoundingly. But still, it was the Tech game, and we had now lost two in a row, again. That is the most we had lost since 1964, but it was never more than two.

Goff was hearing the hounds (no pun intended), but the talent had dropped off some, and he was recruiting well. Wait till next year.

1993 GAME

SCENES FROM 1993 G-DAY GAME, YOURS TRULY AS HONORARY COACH

2012 GAMES

Third generation's first game.

What IS this?

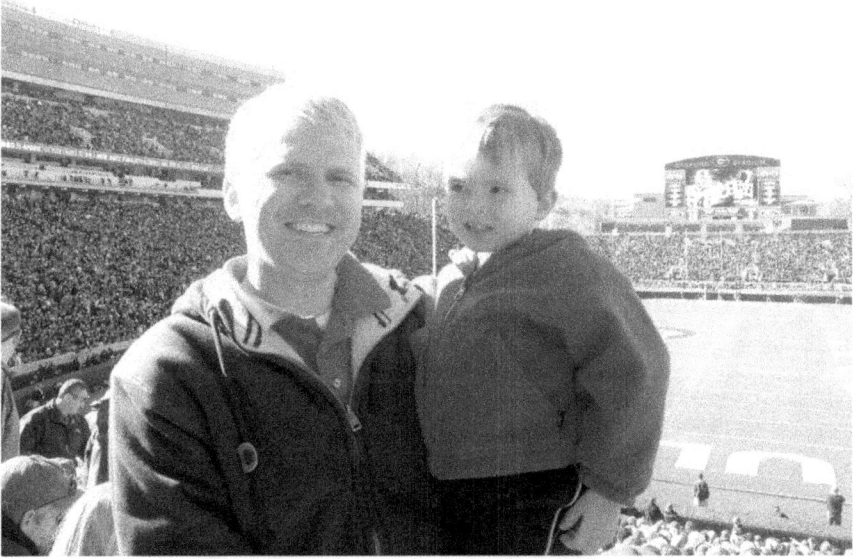

Second and Third generation's first time together.

First but not last time at the Arch.

SCENES FROM THE 2013 GAME

A night game is tough on the little ones.

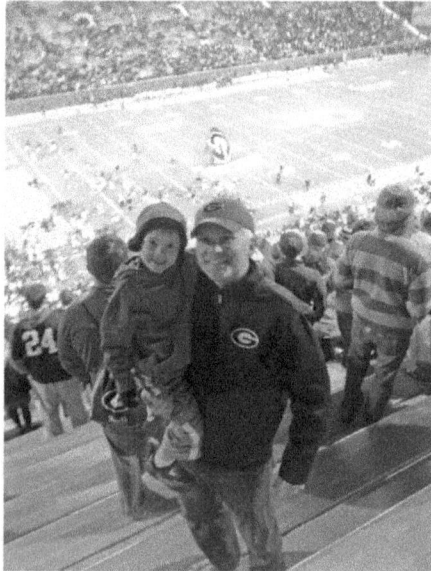

Son and grandson "in heaven."

Bedlam after one of the greatest games ever.

What a game!

2015 GAME

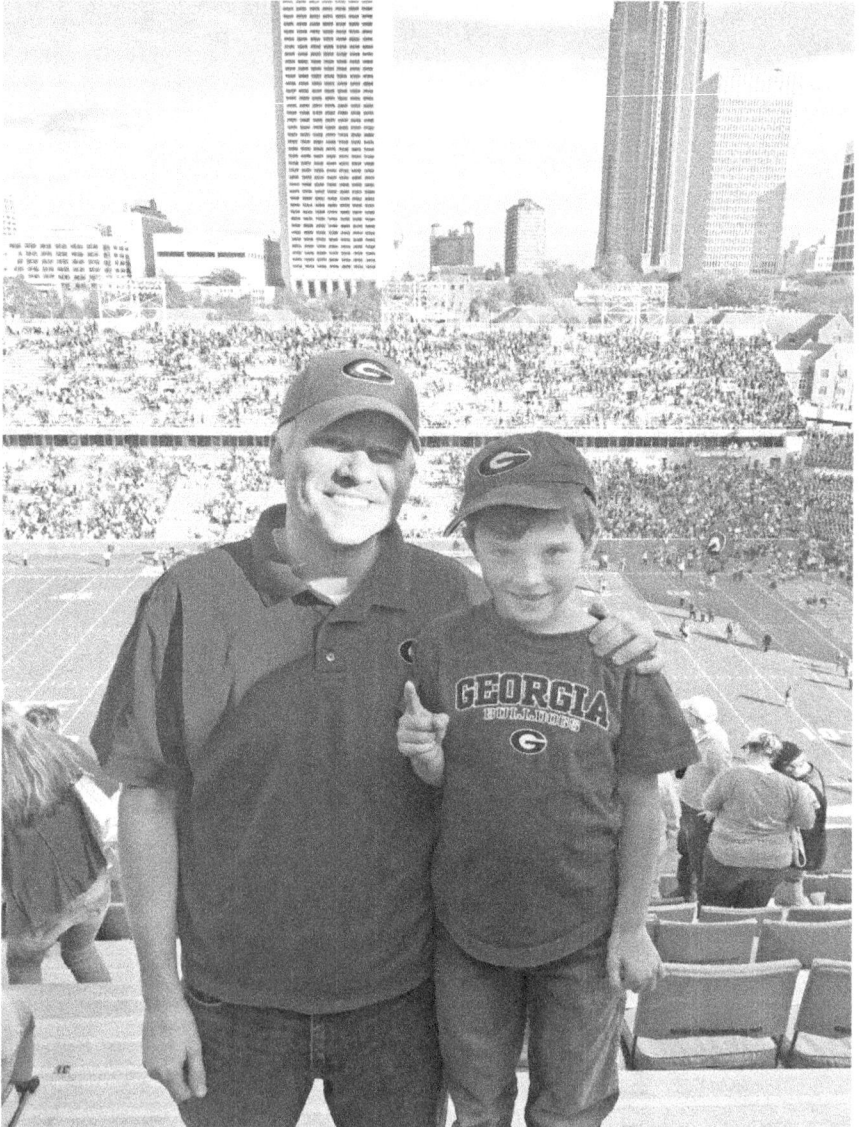

Son and grandson at game I missed while in Italy—breaking the streak at 50!.

1991

HERE IT IS…next year. Ga. has a very good year, their best since 1988. They accomplished the following tasks. They beat LSU but lost a heartbreaker to Alabama, 10-0. They beat #6 Clemson, #23 Ole Miss, and Auburn. They entered the Tech game 7-3.

Tech has a rough follow-up year to their national champ season. They are at one point 2-3. They enter the last game because they played an extra game, 7-4.

Ga. has Hearst again but also a quarterback for the first time in a few years, Eric Zeier, along with other offensive stars Andre Hastings and Mack Strong. Their defense is good.

We leave for Grant Field full of trepidation, however. This is the defending national champion team at their home, and we had been down. The thought of losing three in a row was nerve-wracking. Remember, we had never done that since I had been following from the early sixties.

We had to do it—win—before the feeling could be restored.

We sat in the boxes on the south side, and it was a blissful game. Ga. won 18-15, but it was really not that close. Hearst broke a long run and all of a sudden I felt a calmness that the game was in hand. Tech moved the ball but could never get that score that drew them even.Georgia's defense played well, the best in a couple of years, and the flow was decidedly controlled by Ga.

Order had been restored in the universe, at least in a football universe in the state of Georgia.

Ray Goff, who had become a good friend, was on cloud nine. It was his first victory over Tech as a coach. We met on the field after the game. I thought he would crush me when he hugged me. Even with poor teams, he would never lose to Tech

71

again. As a player and coach, he was 8-3, and as a player, he was 3-1.

Tech still had Shawn Jones at quarterback, but they were not the same team. I don't know why....and I really don't care! The drop off is curious, however. It would get worse and then Ross would be gone. I think it shows how precarious the program is at Tech, in terms of recruiting, media coverage, fan support, and all the rest. It is always walking a tightrope between establishing a solid foundation and simply going from year to year.

They did go on to win their bowl game and finish 8-5, while Ga. beat Arkansas in a bowl to finish 9-3 and a final ranking of #17. It was a pretty good turn around.

1992

IT WAS GOFF'S BEST team and one that co-shared the SEC East crown, although their overall record was two games better than co-champ Florida. This was a team that beat Ohio State in a bowl; a team that would finish 10-2 and be ranked #8; a team that beat Tech 31-17. Garrison Hearst would rush for over 1,500 yards and finish third in the Heisman voting. Eric Zeier would pass for over 2,200. They beat Ohio State in the bowl game 21-14. This team finished 9th in the country in points scored and 3rd in points yielded! It was a truly great team that, because it did not win the conference, is seen as average and not one of the best ever.

Tech was in its first year under Bill Lewis who, ironically, was a former defensive coach at UGA. He actually was the one who succeeded Erk Russell when he left for Ga. Southern. He, Coach Lewis, whose son went to and played at UGA, was head of recruiting in the metro Atlanta area, and back then people like me could help in the effort. I got to know him while helping with that, and I thought, and still think, the world of him. But as we will see, it did not work out for him at Tech. Tech in 1992 finished 5-6, and that would be the best they would do under Lewis.

This game was over probably before kickoff. The score, while not close, was not indicative of the game. It was actually much worse! UGA ran and passed at will, and Tech scored late to close the gap somewhat. This was a great Ga. team. They lost by 2 points to Florida and by 3 to UT in Athens and quarterback Heath Schuler, a future congressman from Tennessee.

Again, I was on the sideline while my sons sat in the stands in our seats. Goff was now 2-2 as the coach against Tech and had the program headed in the right direction…or did he?

Around this time, I had an incredible experience. I will be honest and tell you I do not remember exactly which year it is, but I have pictures to prove it. It was in 1993 or 1994.

Because of my job, I had become friends with Billy Payne, the head of the Atlanta Olympic movement. I had done a number of things for him and he was always more appreciative of it than I thought necessary, but we were very appreciative of each other.

During that "era", when the spring game was held, they were coached by "coaches" who were guests brought in by the staff and the Athletic Director, Vince Dooley. They were celebrities really. Remember, Billy had made All-Sec under Dooley.

Well, Billy was asked to be the coach of one of the teams, and I think Rankin Smith of the other. Billy, amazingly, asked me to assist him as the assistant coach! I was flabbergasted. We had a blast. It was a memory of a lifetime.

Back to the game.

Tech had experienced another down time in recruiting. The play on the field reflected that. Ga. was clearly superior in talent; however, Tech fought hard, which was not always the case. Ga. amassed a lot of yards—over 400—during the game.

It is hard to assess, when you look at the years as they pass by, how Tech can go from very good to very bad and back again in such a short period of time. Is coaching more important there than at other places? "Experts" say the better talent you have, the less need for a great technical coach. I don't know. All I know is after watching so many games, you realize there are a lot of highs and lows in a quick time span with Tech. Their claim to fame in this game was the band! It put a Yellow Jacket tarp over the "G" at midfield. Such immaturity.

1993

THIS TEAM AND THIS YEAR are hard to figure out. They start out 1-4, then win the next three to even up their record, then lose a close one to Florida in the rain and then to Auburn. Tech meanwhile goes 5-6 again. But heading into this game, they have a chance to have a winning record with a victory over UGA at Grant Field. They get beat 43-10! It's hard to figure out both teams, but especially Tech. (See above regarding "hard to figure out" and "fighting hard.")

This game, played at noon on Thanksgiving Day, is a runaway. You might guess by the score, but it incrementally became that. As the score by Ga. mounted, Tech got frustrated and fights broke out on the field everywhere. Goff could be seen throwing his players off the pile of bodies that were scrumming. It was not a good sight for either side to witness. The Georgia players later said Tech was just going over the line of sportsmanship, play after play, and it finally built up.

I am up in the stands with my youngest on the east side near the north end zone, so I have a clear and close view of the fighting. After the game, I go onto the track around the stands and Goff brings us onto the field, and we walk with him to the dressing room. I pointed out how he was throwing the players off, and he looked at me incredulously and said, "Really, I didn't realize that!" He is a big man, but adrenaline is amazing!

At this juncture, upon reflection, it was becoming obvious that UGA's football program was pulling ahead of Tech's. Even in "down" years, there is a difference. In "up" years there is a huge difference. A clear pattern is taking place. At that point, however, I am not sure why. But it will start to become clearer later, and I will talk about that as it develops.

UGA now has a three-game winning streak, but the program overall is at a crossroads. And we know it.

Georgia should have had a better record and, even with losing Hearst early along with others, there was enough talent to have a better season. But the Tech game was one of the better ones, if you believe in the "routs are better than nail biters" philosophy. Goff now had a winning record against Tech as a coach.

1994

THINGS ARE NOT ANY BETTER for Ga.—actually, they have gotten worse. They are worse, in my opinion, for several reasons. Allow me to elaborate. Ga. has a 6-4-1 record with another victory over Tech, but they are 3-4 in conference with a one-point loss to Alabama. This is a loss that absolutely should not have happened. A horrible call by an official allowed Alabama to win. Even then, we had the ball and needed only a few yards for a first down, which would ice the game. We did not get it. A loss to Vanderbilt and Florida followed. They did have a seminal "victory" over an undefeated Auburn. I say a victory, though really it was a tie, in Auburn. Auburn had an undefeated streak going and was ranked #3 in the country at the time. I was there with friends and my son, and it was a great game. I went to the locker room afterward. More on that later. So, going into the Tech game, Ga. is 5-4-1.

The Vandy defeat and subsequent narrow victory over Kentucky had the Bulldog fans up in arms, especially after the season they had the previous year. Ga. had some talent but not so much on defense. Plus, they had gone through a couple of defensive coordinators. The fans had turned on Ray Goff and were not giving him any benefit of the doubt. Things I heard in the stands were hurtful, especially since a lot of them were directed at his being a southerner and a simple (meaning "no airs") man. I could identify with that and took umbrage at that elitist attitude. The student body was changing. The fact is, the entire state of Georgia was changing rapidly, but that is something to be written about by a political scientist. Oh, right—I was and am one! Maybe later.

It was obvious Ga. was not going to a bowl, even with a winning record. (The bowl explosion had not started yet.) But there was still Tech.

Tech, meanwhile, was in even more turmoil. Bill Lewis started 1-7 with a narrow defeat against #7 Arizona to start the season. He had one victory over a Division II school. He was fired during the season (never a good thing for the team!) and replaced by George O'Leary, who went 0-3 the rest of the way. Tech went 1-11 overall.

Ga. wins even bigger than the year before, 48-10.

In Athens, it is a brawl (but not the kind we saw in Atlanta last year), a one-sided brawl. We are in our season ticket seats in the east end zone (though I started out on the sideline) so we can see, somewhat, when the visiting team comes in and out of their dressing room. They looked really down and I *almost* felt sorry for the program. There's not much to tell about this game—same as the year before. What are highlights in a beating like this? The game did end with a dramatic turn, however. Eric Zeier tore his leg up and Mike Bobo, a redshirt freshman, came in and finished the game. It was kind of a microcosm of the last couple of years.

Back to the Auburn game.

It is during this time that Will Muschamp played for UGA. He was Zeier's roommate, as a matter of fact. He is from my hometown of Rome, and I played under his father, Larry. I used to go to their house and visit during my college years and beyond. They are a great family. I used to watch Will run around in his diapers! So, during this time period, and being friends with Goff, I was able to chat with Will off and on, even during the games. After the Auburn game that I mentioned earlier, the group of us who went over for the game went to the locker room to celebrate. I saw Will's Dad, my former coach, and we all had a great conversation.

Back to the Tech game. The game starts out somewhat close, and I go up to Will on the bench while the offense is on the field. I say, "Will, please don't let these guys hang around. You can go undefeated against them." Will says, "Don't worry, Mr. Anthony, we got this. They will not win. I'm not going to ever lose to them!" And he didn't.

1995

THIS IS GETTING TO BE REDUNDANT. Georgia has an up-and-down year. They enter the Tech game 5-5. They lose by 3 to UT, by 8 to Ole Miss, and are blown out by Alabama and Florida. Then they lose to Auburn by 6. By this time, they are down to their fourth-string quarterback. Mike Bobo, a sophomore, got hurt earlier in the year. It was kind of poetic, as he subbed for Zeir the year before when he got hurt. Then what happens but the second stringer himself gets hurt. At that point, a player who had never really played the position since high school had to man the position, a fellow by the name of Hines Ward, a sophomore. We also lost one of the better running backs in UGA history, Robert Edwards.

Tech's record is not much better. They enter 6-4.They improve significantly in the conference, posting a winning 5-3 record for the first time in years.

The weather in Atlanta for the game is overcast, and, if I remember correctly, it drizzled some. I was on the sideline, and my son was in the stands with others. It was at noon on Thanksgiving.

UGA wins 18-17. Hines Ward shows, I think in this game more than any other, what an amazing athlete he is. First off, he was beaten to death in every play yet never slowed down. He passed, he ran and he kept Ga. in the game enough to get in range for the winning field goal. He was 11-11 in third-down passes and was 22-33 overall. The defense, of course, played great and without their effort the low score would not have been enough. Ward said later that he hated being put in that position but realized, in the long run, it made him a better player, especially in his professional career!

It is truly another strange game. The Bulldogs played their heart out. Goff had been *fired* earlier the week before but would be allowed to coach this game and a possible bowl. They had to play their best, as was evident, partly because of the injuries and partly because Tech was as good as or better than UGA....at least in this game. I think this was the most satisfying win for Goff, but from the outside, all one saw was another poorly played game by both teams.

These recent years, in the mid-nineties I think, set back the series! Neither team was on the national radar. Tech had fallen drastically from '90 and '91. UGA had only one great year, 1992, and one good year, 1991, in the entire decade until 1997.

It was punctuated for me when Ray called me the day Vince fired him. That, also, is another book for someone to write.

Back to the game. UGA dominated the time of possession but had little to show for it, especially in the first half. By early in the second half, they were down 0-14. Then they scored twice and went for two the second time after Tech added a field goal. Down 15-17, they get the ball inside their 15 with about 7 minutes left in the game and drive all the way down for a Kanon Parkman field goal of about 34 yards. It shows that even poorly played and otherwise boring games can have a great deal of excitement when the score stays close. This one was a nail biter. I was on the sidelines for most of the game, and when it was over, I was swamped by fans and players and made my way to Goff for a big hug, for the last time.

1996

JIM DONNAN IS THE NEW COACH, after Glen Mason reneges (very embarrassing, especially with his pronunciation of Bulldogs!) on a hiring, and things get worse from there.

Georgia goes into the Tech game 4-6, and they win 19-10 to still finish under .500. They start out the season losing to Southern Mississippi and South Carolina, later to Kentucky, and then by 40 to #1 Florida. They do beat Auburn, there, in their first overtime game (this is the game from which the famous picture of UGA (our mascot) attacking the Auburn player came). This is the game where Mike Bobo comes off the bench (Donnan did not think he was good enough to start) and rallied the team to victory. He would be the quarterback until he finished his career.

Tech is not much better. They come into the game 5-5, so if they win, even being in Athens, they have a winning season. They had lost to Navy just before this game, but they did beat #13 Virginia earlier in the season. Joe Hamilton is their freshman quarterback.

It was another stinker of a game. Going in I am nervous because when both teams are bad, weird things can happen, and the bottom line is I want a victory—who cares how bad they are? From a distance and retrospective view, the series and the programs, together, were about as bad as they had been in decades. I remember sitting in our seats in the east end zone and thinking that neither team deserved to win.

Consider this. In the nineties, through seven seasons, this is what we have. Tech, with a national championship in one year, a good season in another, one 6-5 season, and the rest under (and sometimes way under) .500.

Georgia had one great year, one good year, one .500 season, one winning (6-4-1) season, and the rest under .500. Between the two teams, half the years were under .500.

But as I said, a victory over Tech is a victory over Tech! It goes in the record books as such and is counted in the "plus" column.

Going into 1997, neither program could be considered one of the top 30 in the country. That is about to change, in some ways very dramatically.

1997

UGA REBOUNDS with a 10-2 record. But again, it was a very uneven performance. They lose in Knoxville to #9 UT by 25, and to #11 Auburn in Athens by 11. They beat #6 Florida by 20! Then in the bowl, they dismantle Wisconsin by 27. Nevertheless, it was the best record since 1992 and second best since the glorious early eighties, and consequently, they wind up being ranked #10.

They are loaded with talent, and much of it came from 4th and 5th-year seniors.

Tech, meanwhile, posts a winning season, goes to a bowl and wins it to finish 7-5. They have Joe Hamilton as a sophomore.

While going to Grant Field, however, I am worried that their up-and-down season is better than ours. They lose to #11 Notre Dame by 4. Then they beat #17 Clemson, but they also lose to #3 FSU by 5 touchdowns, to #5 N. Carolina, and then beat the rest of the teams they should beat. Tech finishes #25 in the country. It's their first ranking in six years.

A large group of us go and we split up for our seats. My son and I and a friend and his brother-in-law are in the extreme corner of the west stands, first row, on the wall. The wives sit in the new enclosed section in the south stands. That is done for several reasons, but mostly because it was going to rain. Rain it did, off and on during the whole game.

This is one of the ten, if not five, best games ever. Ga. wins 27-24 (of course, or I would not have said it was one of the best games ever in the rivalry).

Here is how it unfolds. It is somewhat of a back-and-forth game, but Ga. is in control to a large extent. They open a 21-10 lead midway through the third quarter. Defense is playing well, holding Tech to a couple of field goals overall. Our offense gets stymied several times. Early in the fourth, UGA leads 21-16. Tech punts UGA deep, they cannot move, and Tech gets the ball on Georgia's 45. We hold them, though, and they punt again. They hold and we punt, and they get the ball at midfield with five minutes and thirty-five seconds to go in game. We stop them again. They punt us deep again and we only get to our 16, so we punt to our 48-yard line. There are now only two minutes and sixteen seconds left in the game.

Tech runs I think one or two plays, but on third down, they have Hamilton on the run fifteen yards behind the line of scrimmage in their grasp. He gets out and passes to a receiver who gets to the sixteen. They score several plays later, on fourth down, with 48 seconds on the clock. They go for two and make that! Tech is ahead 24-21.

I remember to this day how I felt. This was something we usually did to them. I was so mad at Donnan, though I don't know why (at that point he had not done anything egregious). I just could not fathom how we could cough up a victory like that. In my time, I had never experienced that type of game from our perspective. It was to serve as a precursor for his time there.

But we get the ball on the 35, courtesy of an out of bounds kickoff, the fourth in the game by both teams. We have two timeouts, remember—forty-eight seconds!

It was the first play: a tunnel screen to Champ Bailey, primarily a defensive back who goes on to a stellar pro career. He is one of the best players in Ga. history. Because of the tunnel screen, he goes from the 35 to Tech's 37. There are only forty seconds left.

Second play. They pass to Bailey again, and he gets to the 30. Thirty-five seconds left.

Third play. Pass to Robert Edwards who gets to the 22 with 21 seconds left. First down.

Fourth play. Pass over the middle; they intercept. Flag thrown. Tech interference. Ball on the 9 with 14 seconds left. First down.

Fifth play. Bobo to Allen in the corner of the southeast end zone, as far away from us as can be. TOUCHDOWN!

But we did not know at first instance. I looked at the UGA fans that always sit in that corner, and as I watched them I knew. At that point we all were going crazy! My son came to hug me (he is 19 then) and breaks my nose. Then he flips over the wall, unintentionally, and joins in the celebration. He reminded me of me in 1971!

There were eight seconds left in the game. We get penalties for excessive celebration (players or fans?) so our extra point is from the 32. We do not make it. So that is the final score: 27-24.

I also remember how I felt then: pure jubilation and satisfaction. I had forgotten all about the other series of bad plays. As I said, it was one of the best games ever.

But after reflection a few days later, it was obvious Tech was improving tremendously. That was one of the confusing attributes of sitting there watching them come back. They had not shown that type of play for years. I knew the series had tightened up, but more impressively, there were two good teams on the field for a change.

Anyway, UGA now has a seven-game win streak and we have them in Athens the next year.

1998

LET ME START OFF BY SAYING this up front: the next three years are THE WORST! UGA loses three in a row to Tech for the first time since the early sixties. Donnan is eventually fired for this and other issues. They also lose a bunch of other meaningful games. O'Leary proves to be more than a match for Donnan and is hired, mostly because of this success, by Notre Dame. (The fact that he never coaches there is another story. There are a lot of subplots with this series.)

Yes, we are robbed twice, once as blatantly as can be. But that is no excuse—the games should not have been that close. The 2000 game is one of the worst defeats of UGA ever. By the point difference, it is not, but by the performance it is.

So let's start with 1998. The Bulldogs wind up ranked 14th in the country with a 9-3 record. They beat #6 LSU but lose to conference champ Tennessee, #4 at the time. Then they lose to #6 Florida and #17 Tech, 21-19. UGA is ranked 12th at the time of the Tech game.

This starts the Quincy Carter Era, such as it was. You can have him back, Tech, drugs and all.

Tech, on the other hand, winds up ranked 9th and is 10-2 after their bowl victory. They lose to Boston College and #6 FSU, but beat #17 Notre Dame, #7 Virginia, #23 North Carolina State and, as I said, #12 UGA. They put together two five-game winning streaks. They are conference co-champs. They *are* good.

Nevertheless, I feel the Bulldogs should win going in, and not without merit. I am, of course, very worried and nervous, but I do not see any mismatch. It is in Athens, and another group of us go together. We had to get extra tickets, so we all sit in those seats, which are in the first row of the upper deck on the extreme corner of the southeast stands. It is an interesting angle and view, one I had never experienced in Sanford Stadium—and I must say, I really liked it. We even had VIP parking to go with the tickets.

It is a very close game, several lead changes with turnovers by both teams but more by UGA. After all is said and done, we have the lead late and Tech starts a drive. Hamilton is running on a keeper, he is tackled near the Tech bench and fumbles. However, the refs do not call it that way. There was no replay back then. (See 1999.) They continue to march and with a minute left, they call a timeout to set a play on 3rd and ten. They complete a rather long pass for a first down.

Tech keeps the ball and at the five-second mark, they call a timeout to kick a field goal to go for the win. Tech is successful on the kick from 35 yards with two seconds left, and UGA loses.

The Ga. defense actually played well, but the offense sputtered. In the fourth quarter alone, Ga. had the ball three times and ran a total of nine plays for 14 yards! One, maybe two, first downs along the way and Tech would have run out of time. This was a pitiful performance after getting 19 points and 278 total yards throughout three quarters. Earlier we missed on a two-point attempt.

We all felt somewhat like it was payback for the year before. By losing, Donnan loses his first to Tech. It will not be his last. We saw a familiar pattern emerging under Donnan—good offensive scheme, but poorly executed when crunch time comes. Many of us come to think it is because of the type of athletes he is recruiting and how he treats them. They're too undisciplined and there is no demand for accountability. But at that moment, and looking forward to the next year, one has a way of ignoring the obvious. Many times the obvious becomes so only in retrospect.

Still, after all that, Ga. loses by only two. Even teams, even performances, and even breaks; Tech just got the last one.

1999

BOTH TECH AND GEORGIA wind up this season going 8-4. Ga. enters the Tech game 7-3; Tech enters 7-3. Tech loses their bowl; Ga. wins theirs.

Georgia loses to Florida, Auburn and Tech. Remember what I said of the 1975 team, how they were "champions" for beating Florida, Auburn and Tech? It was just the opposite with this team.

Tech loses to #1 FSU, Wake Forest, Virginia and Miami in the bowl. They were not very intimidating.

UGA is ranked ahead of Tech, and we are back in Atlanta. It is a beautiful, sunny day and not too cold, but crisp. We are sitting in the east stands lower deck but under the "famous" overhang and in front of one of the even more famous columns used to hold up the oldest stadium in America. There is a group of us including my wife and I, my youngest son, and another couple, who also brought along the woman's brother. We are surrounded by Tech fans.

The game is back and forth, mainly because neither defense is very good. Every possession seems like it leads to a score. UGA loses its best defensive player early in the game while he is playing offense! It is high scoring and exciting from that standpoint, but it is frustrating to watch. When both teams amass an astounding 62 first downs, you know there is no defense. Ga. had 547 total yards of offense and Tech had 550. Even with overtime, this is a vast amount of offensive yardage. We Ga. fans felt like Tech should be put away, but it could not be done. As a matter of fact, Georgia is down ten, 41-31, at the start of fourth quarter. Several bad calls, a couple in Georgia's favor, occur throughout. Georgia eventually ties the game. Then Tech scores,

UGA scores again, and with a few minutes left the Bulldogs are driving. The game is tied again.

They are driving late in the game and are inside Tech's five-yard line after a first down run from around the twenty. They give the ball to Jasper Sanks, the highly touted running back, for one more try for a touchdown before settling for a game-clinching field goal. The game is tied. Why not kick the field goal then?

There are 9 seconds left at the snap. Sanks goes up the middle, then fumbles...Or does he? That's what the refs say. Again, this is before replay, but in subsequent replays from TV, it clearly shows he had been down for some time. Gary Danielson says so; writers the next day say so. Later, much later, even the Tech people admitted they stole one, courtesy of the refs. The coaches, the announcer..."My God," as Munson would say, "The absolute worst ever."

So we go to overtime, the first in the series' history. I do not like overtimes. There are too many variables that you cannot control. I did not know what to think of this one, being the first, so I had neither a good nor bad premonition.

Ga. gets the ball first and Carter throws a horrible interception. It's not that any were actually good, but he did this all the time—trying to make an impossible pass while ignoring other open receivers. So Tech gets the ball and positions themselves for a field goal on third down. Ga. blocks it but Tech recovers and gets another chance. They make this one and win, 51-48.

A disgusting end. A Tech fan in front of us turns around and says to me with a smirk on his face and knowing we are for Georgia, "Good game, huh?" I tell him to go to hell. My wife is horrified. It will be the last Tech-Ga. game she ever goes to with me, or with anyone else for that matter.

Sorry, but that is the attitude that I described at the beginning of this tale regarding Tech's attitude toward us, and it brought back a lot of childhood memories. It was a spontaneous reaction that should have been a little more muted and which I should not have made, but the emotions were running high. I was not mad at Tech so much as at the refs and the UGA team.

A few months later we were at a function, and Barbara and Vince were there and we were talking. This game came up and my wife recounted this story. Vince looks at her and says, "So what's the problem?" She rolled her eyes and said something to the effect, "I should have guessed you would agree." Barbara chuckles.

After the previous year, I really started believing in fate. To lose two games in a row in the manner they were lost was eerie. To play below par and still have a chance at victory was frustrating. To see the undisciplined nature of the team under Donnan was embarrassing. Tech had improved tremendously under O'Leary, make no mistake. But Ga., given their natural advantages, was still in a position to win both games. Again, it cannot be emphasized enough. Tech only wins under a few scenarios. When they are clearly better, as do most teams; when Ga. is down, regardless of Techs year and when Ga. gives them the game when being the favorite.

2000

TECH IS ON A TWO-GAME win streak and is having another good season. They come to Athens 8-2, having lost to FSU and NC State. They reeled off seven victories in a row. Ga. is 7-3, having lost, again, to Florida, Auburn and Tech. They do win their bowl, which was small consolation. Tech loses theirs, by the way, to LSU.

The weather is bad—rainy, chilly—and the entire mood of the Bulldog nation is palpably down. In the stands, in conversations, looking at the bench—everywhere you could determine the mood was there. I have never seen it so bad. It must have been what it was like just before Vince came in November, 1963.

So, you ask, did I think we could win? For the first time since 1990, I had my serious doubts. After sitting in the stands for about half of the first quarter, I really came to the conclusion that we would be lucky to win. This had to stop, and a change had to be made.

I know this sounds like sour grapes, but there is not a lot to say about this game from a Bulldog viewpoint. They beat us with a good defense and a serviceable quarterback who plays like a good one. Maybe Ga. had something to do with that. It became obvious as the game wore on that Tech would win and Ga. was somewhere else mentally. It was miserable. In my mind, I think it was the closest to the 1974 game that I could remember. And that was not a good memory. The final score was 27-15, but it was really not that close. How Georgia was losing was what made these seasons so bad. The records were good on paper and resembled some of Dooley's records. But the difference is…What are you getting out of your talent?

Did Ga. have talent? Yes, so much so that before the season, Donnan said this is the type of team he always dreamed of coaching. Did Tech have talent? Absolutely. Did we give them the game? Not really. They whipped Ga. in every phase of the game, along the lines of the 1990 game. So Ga. is down, not from a talent level, but from an attitude and execution/coaching standpoint. A change has to be made. We'd seen three Tech victories in a row—the first time since the early sixties, almost forty years ago!

But first the game. Going in, I repeat, the records were virtually even, with Ga. playing a tougher schedule. They had underachieved, but they could still beat Tech. Only when I saw that their attitude matched the weather did I realize they would not win. Over these fifty years, I would say that this game saw the worst domination of Georgia by Tech, with a resultant victory, equal to or worse than 1974 and 1990. Therefore, it ranks in the top three worst games ever by Ga. The past two games we played below par but could have and should have won. There was no doubt on this one that Ga. got whipped physically, mentally, and coaching-wise, and was intimidated on top of that. That makes it the worst game ever, in my opinion. We need to move on.

2001

AND SO WE DO. Donnan is fired and a new coach is brought in. Nobody ever said Donnan could not recruit. Some of them were not the best students or persons of high moral character, but they had talent. Mark Richt takes those same players and fashions an 8-4 season, a good turnaround. How is that a turnaround? For starters, they beat Tech, 31-12, in Atlanta. They beat #7 Tennessee, "hobbed nail boot" game. And for the first time in a while, they have what appears to be a legitimately good quarterback, freshman David Greene. There are other good young ones also. Those young players are balanced by the likes of Musa Smith and Verron Haynes.

Tech finishes 8-5, another one of those strange years with an extra game. Both teams enter the game 7-3. Tech won their bowl; Ga. did not. Tech is ranked #21 at the time—another strange occurrence. O'Leary leaves after the season but before the bowl game for Notre Dame. Mac McWhorter, a former UGA player and coach, who is on the staff, coaches the bowl game and they win, as I said, under a Bulldogs coach. Tech loses another good coach in his prime.

My youngest and I go to a Bulldog Club reception (the game is at night) before the game, and the talk is really depressing. It is somewhere between fatalistic and apprehension about what the new guy can pull off. Until it is done, we all are in a loser's mindset. I remember walking over to Grant Field, on a cold, crisp, clear night and just wondering, *Will it ever end?*

It does. Ga. starts off like gangbusters, running the ball relentlessly at Tech. Tech, meanwhile, can muster nothing on offense the entire night. Ga. scores often and Tech gets one score by the half. By early in the second half, it is obvious that UGA

93

will win and the mood improves significantly. We are in seats in the upper deck in the west stands, and it is a pretty good view. Not many other Bulldogs fans are around, but there are a few and we do not really start acting like we have this won until the fourth quarter. We have been burned too much lately to feel otherwise. It was as festive a game and feeling as I could remember in a long time. I am assuming it was one gigantic exhale of relief and a feeling that order had been restored. At that moment, Mark Richt could have run for governor and won. Because of all the young talent, the future looked bright and we left there already looking ahead to the next year.

2002

THE NEXT YEAR; what a year! One of the best in UGA history. They win the SEC championship by beating Arkansas in the championship game. They lose only to Florida by a touchdown. They have other good victories over four ranked teams, including a thriller over Alabama, there. They beat Tech 51-7 in Athens, which at that point was the largest margin of victory in the history of the series. It cannot get much better than that. They are ranked third in the country at the end of the season.

Tech, meanwhile, has a new coach, Chan Gailey, a native Georgian from Americus. They go 7-6 but are 7-4 coming to Athens.

I must tell the truth, I was not really worried about this game. I knew UGA could lose, but I knew it was highly unlikely. Just as in a few of the other years, you come to the stadium with a little bit lighter step, and the jokes are funnier.

We are in our season ticket seats in the east end zone, and it is a track meet—except the Bulldogs are the only ones running. The sun is partially hidden, but there is enough sun to say it is a bright and sunny day. There is not much more one can say about a game like this, where the score is so decisive and the outcome is over after the first quarter, 24-0.

I had a feeling after it was over, and it was much different from some of those blowout games in the nineties. In those games in the nineties under Goff, you had, or at least I had, a sense that there was an emptiness of accomplishment. Beating a team, any team, that bad, several years in a row, creates a feeling that it was not enough, a feeling that there has really not been any type of accomplishment after all.

That is not how I felt after this one. I enjoyed it, savored it and felt that "let's have more like this" feeling. That is what losing three in a row will do to you.

2003

SO THIS YEAR UGA wins 34-17. Looks like a closer game, but it really was not any more competitive than before.

Yes, Ga. was really good again, winning the eastern division, and Tech ultimately had a 7-6 record. But that is the issue: there is a world of difference between teams with those three loss differences. Georgia beat Alabama again but lost to Florida and LSU twice, the last time being in the championship game. The first time was in a heartbreaker in Baton Rouge, in a disputed call and resultant TD by LSU, who would go on to win the national championship, the first by Nick Saban.

This Tech game, of course, is in Atlanta. The Bulldogs are ranked #5 coming in. It is a cold, crisp, sunny day and a group of us, family, all go together. We, minus my wife, are sitting in those seats, more or less, that we sat in for the 1999 game, the one where my wife said she would never come to another game. I have the same feeling again, that there's no way Georgia should lose. Even losing to LSU, Georgia wins their bowl, finish 11-3 and are ranked #7.

As last year, there is not much to say other than the Tech team seemed to show more fight and spirit. When I say "fight" I mean it literally, as that seems to be the case every few years. There were eight late hits and unsportsmanlike conduct penalties, five by UGA. But the worst is their freshman quarterback, Reggie Ball, who hit the Ga. trainer. Shortly after, he goes to the locker room and comes out for the second half with shoulder pads off, and the announcer says he has suffered a concussion. Yeah right! All who believe that, raise your hand. We knew what happened, and I actually had respect for Coach Gailey.

Tech does put up a better effort, but they just do not have the same talent. The game is close for a while, even with Ga. jumping to a quick 14-0 lead. The second half is mostly a party for Bulldog fans. On we go to the next year in terms of how we view playing Tech. We start to feel like we are on another of those long victory runs. There are only two questions—will games be competitive? And where will we finish in the national picture?

2004

THE PARTY CONTINUES, or does it? We get a competitive game.

UGA wins only 19-14 in a thrilling game, in Athens no less. The game is fiercely fought and right down to the wire. It is as close as the score indicates.

UGA is ranked #7 coming in, and Tech is unranked. We are in our season seats and getting drenched. My old hat is taking a beating. (This hat used to play "Glory, Glory" when you mashed a button. That stopped years ago. The hat has since been "retired.") The weather is cold and rainy. The rain stops more or less in the second half, but it is still raw and the field is treacherous.

We get a good enough lead, but David Greene breaks his thumb in the first quarter and D.J. Shockley plays most of the rest of the game into the fourth quarter. Not much happens on offense, and it was not all the fault of the quarterback. Georgia has the lead but cannot expand it, and cannot even move the ball for first downs much. The team just seems to be flat. But a game is sixty minutes long, and players have to remember that. Most of the time they do. Unfortunately, most fans do not.

Greene comes back in the fourth quarter to settle things down and pull it out. The winningest quarterback in NCAA history (when he graduated) shows how valuable he is to the team.

Tech meanwhile does just enough to stay within a touchdown. They are driving late in the game and Ball completes a long pass to the Ga. 21. Then he completes a pass on first down for no gain; second down he is sacked for an 11-yard loss. The clock is ticking down to zero as he runs up to the line and spikes the ball—on third down! On fourth down, he goes back to pass, scrambles and has no open receiver, so he throws it out of bounds! He later blames all of that on the refs, and this is after three plays and real time of about three minutes—and all with the help of the coaches to call on and or listen to. It was one of the strangest sequences I have ever seen.

We are glad for the victory but concerned that it was so close. Did the weather conditions, Greene being hurt, it getting old hat beating them, have anything to do with the score? That is what keeps fans talking and coaches up at night. We do question whether we will have a good-enough quarterback for next year. Bottom line, though…We had a winning streak at four.

2005

YES, WE DO have a good-enough quarterback…so much so we win the SEC!

The year starts with a thrashing of Boise State. They come in ranked, riding a wave of support from across the county. Why? Because they always have a good record and yet are not ranked high. Ga. showed why. They do not play anybody game in and game out. Still don't, 2011 notwithstanding.

UGA reels off victories in their first seven games! At that point, they are ranked 4th. Then they go to Florida and lose another heartbreaker. Then they come home and play Auburn, off their feet, but lose on a last-chance bomb that Auburn turns into a touchdown. We do not know it then, but we will see that same play and result a few years later. The next week, South Carolina beats Florida, Ga. beats Kentucky, and they are eastern division champs.

They are ranked 13th as they come to Atlanta to face the number 20th ranked Yellow Jackets. It is a night game, and we are in the lower deck of the south end zone, halfway up and somewhat surrounded by Tech fans. "Chill out," I tell my son.

Tech is 7-3 and UGA is 8-2. Each team scores in the first quarter and then nothing happens until the fourth quarter. It really is a good game but not one I was enjoying. We were flat, and I could not figure out why. Maybe we were lax due to clinching the division and looking ahead to LSU the next week. Who knows? I know the coaches do not.

That SEC championship game has proven to change the psychological dynamics of teams as they play their last game, even when it's against a rival.

The fourth quarter is a high-intensity battle. Ga. finally scores on a nice drive with several good passes by Schockley. Then with 3:18 to go, Tech starts their last drive. They get to the Ga. 11! I am sitting there thinking in two different directions. On the one hand, I am in the moment and on edge with the events unfolding on the field and hoping we hold on. On the other hand, I am wondering how in the world this Tech team is so close and about to send the game into overtime. One thing I am keeping in mind is their quarterback. Remember the last two years? Then it happens! Reggie ball rolls out and Tim Jennings intercepts on the five and returns it to the 30! One minute and eleven seconds left. UGA wins again!

Calvin Johnson, for sure the second-best receiver to ever play at a school in Georgia, has only two catches. UGA, except for the third quarter, dominates the game on the field but not on the scoreboard. They win 14-7.

This is Gailey's best team yet, and it showed. He is still a few players short, including quarterback (pun intended), and on reflection, Ga. did not play that bad. Tech had just improved that much.

By the way, UGA embarrasses LSU the next week to capture the SEC but then loses the Sugar Bowl to wind up 10-3 and ranked #10.

2006

To RECAP, Georgia is on a five-game winning streak, Richt is undefeated against Tech, and this year's game is in Athens at night. Bulldog fans should feel good. Reggie Ball is still their quarterback. But look at the last couple of years' scores. It is tightening up. The chatter in Tech circles is that Gailey is not doing a good job. Yes, he has not beaten Ga., but few coaches did consistently (only one has). UGA has won two conference championships and been in the chase for four of the five during Richt's time.

Nevertheless, I am worried (surprised?) that the trend is moving Tech's way. I'm thinking this is one of those crucial games. Win this year and that makes six in a row, and at that point we are at the juncture where you realize Tech has to win sooner or later or the series becomes "one-sided."

On the other hand, it has become apparent, despite the scores, that these two programs have indeed diverged. They are no longer equal. Georgia's overall success is not matched by Tech's, and the revenues in the athletic accounts are far apart. I, like many people in my age range, know that this feeling between the two schools is so different from earlier decades. When I was starting out in the sixties, they were absolutely viewed as equals. As a matter of fact, Tech felt they were superior on the field (they always feel they are superior in the classroom). Now they are not, and that is why some Tech people feel the way they do, including the Athletic Director at that time. This also refers back to the point I have made several times: it really is embarrassing when Tech does win.

It's game time in Athens. I will give you the score first, just to show how the games have become competitive. Tech still cannot pull off a victory. It was UGA 15, Tech 12. Sounds like 1995.

Tech comes in ranked 16th and UGA comes in unranked. Tech is 9-2 coming in, Ga. is 7-4. There is a distinct feeling that the Bulldog program is superior. Yet, it is close enough in most measurements to know that Tech can win if the Dawgs do not come to play with all they have. Ga. started the season 5-0 but sputtered, losing four of the next five. They beat #5 Auburn in Auburn for the only victory among those five games. But they finished strong. After beating Auburn, they beat Tech and Virginia Tech in the Peach Bowl. Tech, as I mentioned, was 9-2 coming in. They then lost to Ga., Wake Forest in the ACC championship game, and to West Virginia in the Gator Bowl, to lose their last three. So, after all was said and done and the season was over, Tech was 9-5 and Ga. was 9-4.

I point this out at this juncture to make a point. When teams play, of course, they do not know how the season will ultimately unfold. So, sometimes, a victory or defeat may be puzzling at the time it is played, but after the season is over you can see why the team that won did so…maybe. The fact is, despite their records at the time Tech and Georgia played, there was not to be a lot of difference in their ultimate success rate. You did not know this at the time of the game, but it became more obvious afterward. But that is Bulldog fans' concern. There is not a lot of difference, it seems, between the two programs.

In any event, because it was in Athens, because Ball was their leader[2] and Matthew Stafford, by this time, had become the first team quarterback, and because of the difference in their strength of schedules, I actually felt we would win. Yes, it would be a close game, but we would win... That is what happened.

It was a defensive battle that was determined by key turnovers, much as any close game can be described. UGA

---

[2] In four years, Reggie Ball was 0-4, with one TD pass and five interceptions. He completed less than **30%** of his passes. Plus, and worst of all, he showed a total lack of class and leadership. I think, and rightly so, that is why Tech supporters disliked him so much and held Gailey responsible for enabling that type of character for four years. Or…perhaps he just may have been the best Tech had!

recovers a fumble for a TD. They intercept ball twice and hold Tech to two field goals. Meanwhile, Ga. scores two TDs and goes for two once and makes it.

Again, they hold the great Calvin Johnson to two measly catches.

Tech is up 12-7 when Stafford leads a late game march to a score, with 1:54 to go. They go for two to make the score 15-12, UGA.

Then Tech is moving when Ball throws his second interception of the game. The Ga. players say Ball then went kicking and shoving them as he left the field, much like his freshman year.

A thrilling game, yes; more so than we wanted, yes; Tech playing UGA even now, yes. It all made the victory less than compelling and enjoyable.

Again, there's the difference between the Bulldog and Yellow Jacket fan. We are disappointed when we win but do not look good. That is because we expect to win and want a good game as icing on the cake. They expect to lose, and when it is close but they still lose, they feel it has been a good day's work.

2007

THIS IS ONE OF THE BEST, yet strangest seasons ever. Ga. finishes 11-2 and ranked #2 in the final poll. Some say they should have been picked to play for the national championship. They beat #18 Auburn, #9 Florida, finally, and #16 Alabama, not to mention #10 Hawaii in the Sugar Bowl. Based on all this, they are ranked #1 in the pre-season 2008 polls. But back to '07.

Tech comes in 7-4, which makes it really another lackluster year, and it winds up being Gailey's last. They lose to UGA and their bowl game to wind up 7-6. They started off the season beating Notre Dame 33-3, but lose three of the next four. They do have a good defense.

In going back over these years and reviewing stats, it is amazing what struck me. For many, many years, Tech loses their last 2, 3, or 4 games to tarnish what would have been an otherwise good year. They fade, badly. Some of it can be explained by the schedule set-up, but not entirely.

Ga. wins this year's game, 31-17—that's more like it! Truthfully, this team was really good and Tech was down from all the turmoil surrounding Gailey and the Ball era. But, be that as it may, UGA now has a seven-game win streak.

It is a late afternoon game and the temperature is chilly! The game is very close after two quarters. UGA goes up three, then Tech scores. Stafford runs 30 yards for a touchdown, then Tech scores again. We are down 10-14 with about five minutes to go in half. We score with a minute and a half left but miss the extra point...16-14 at the half.

In the second half UGA pulls away, but honestly the game is closer than the score indicates. We are in upper deck in south end zone near west stands. With a lot of Bulldog fans in that area, there is a lot of grumbling.

The second half is even duller, except for a couple of strange plays. Tech intercepts a pass and, on the run, fumbles out of the end zone…Georgia's ball. Later Ga. fumbles a punt and it rolls out of end zone…Georgia's ball.

Meanwhile, on the scoreboard, UGA scores with 1:40 to go in the third quarter, and that makes the score 23-14.

A sidebar to this is the UT vs. Kentucky game. If Kentucky wins (not totally impossible) Ga. wins the division. Tennessee goes out to a lead, but UK catches up and ties it at the end…overtime. Ga. fans are listening and watching this game as much as the one in front of them. You get people yelling out things about that game even as something is going on down below. Sometimes, when Kentucky would score, there would be a yell even when there was nothing going on below…It was about the UT game! UT finally wins in four overtimes 52-50!

Back to the Tech game.

At the start of the fourth quarter, Tech kicks a field goal to make it 23-17. By this time, though, you can tell Ga. is wearing Tech down. The scoring drive at the end of the third was an 85-yard drive with two pass plays totaling 80 yards, one for 55 yards. Then later in the quarter, we start running wild and Thomas Brown scores on a long run. Then Knowshon Moreno gets about 50 yards in the last 5 to 7 minutes.

Seven in a row! Looking back, as I did then when Gailey was in fact fired, the games, except for the '02 game, were competitive, in play and most times in the score. Tech just never could win.

Now we head into next year, knowing a victory in 2008 will tie for the longest streak in the series, a streak unfortunately that Tech holds.

2008

ONE THING THIS SEASON proved and has proven since under Richt, is that Ga. is not a good "frontrunner," even within a season. Put them in the underdog role, put their backs against the wall, however, and they play their best. When expectations are high, they fall flat. They don't just lose by a thin margin; they get embarrassed.

As I mentioned earlier, Ga. is ranked #1 going into the season. They win their first game and drop in the rankings! It's not fair or rational, but it goes downhill from there. They start strong, even going to Arizona and beating Arizona State. They come home the next week and get absolutely embarrassed by #8 Alabama, 41-30. However, the game was not near as close as the score seems to show.

They recover, somewhat. (And I still say to this day, the game in Arizona took it out of them physically. I was there, and that heat is indescribable even when you are in it.) They win their next three then get crushed by #5 Florida. They do beat a good #11 LSU team in Baton Rouge. They enter the Tech game ranked 13th.

Tech enters ranked 18th. They are 8-3, not much different than under Gailey.

The game is during the day—cold, wet, and no sun. Paul Johnson is the new coach with his "unique" offense. There had been a lot of chatter about it, and it had been more of a curiosity than an actually effective weapon against good teams. Tech loses to N. Carolina, Virginia and Virginia Tech. (They lose to LSU in the Peach Bowl later.) Their defense is so-so, not nearly as good as it had been in the last couple of years under Gailey.

Ga. starts strong. Stafford throws one of his patented interceptions for a touchdown. Ga. scores 28 points though, in one half. All in all, it is a very good half with a lot of offense, and the defense allows only one touchdown. Tech goes for two twice and fails both times. Why they went for two after the first touchdown is beyond me. It was probably Johnson trying to be a big shot.

It is harrowing to watch their offense, but you have to adjust your expectations. They will win the battle of possession and they will get yards. The name of the game, though, is still who has the most points. More on their offense later.

So, at halftime, I am actually thinking that his offense (Johnson's) is not all that great for scoring; with our 28 points, I know we will score more, so we are in good shape. I was steamed at the interception and remarked to my son when it happened, "Hope that is not the difference in the game." Of course, as you know, it was. No excuse. Gunslingers get killed, and when a quarterback has that mentality, he kills his team!

The third quarter is a dream…actually a nightmare. Tech scores 26 unanswered points. That is not good, but the game was lost by the offense doing absolutely nothing. One little meager score would have made all the difference. The offense that scored 28 points in the first half is shut down in the third quarter.

Tech scores three TDs and one field goal, two successful two-point tries. Twenty-six points!

Ga. scores two more times in the fourth quarter; Tech scores once more. Ga. never pulls even. So with 4:04 to go in the game Tech gets the ball and is ahead 45-42. Ga. never sees the ball again.

It was an absolutely disgusting game, a rare loss, and, as is the case so many times, one Georgia should have and could have won. Yes, Tech played well. They cannot win if they do not play well. But Georgia has to play bad (when they are the favorite to win) to lose. That is what happened. Count the mistakes, count the futile times on offense, count the missed tackles…Oh heck, just stop counting.

2009

LET ME SAY, without a doubt of reservation or contradiction, this game's outcome was the most savoring, most rewarding and by far most gratifying victory I ever experienced. Then and still to this day.

It was exciting, but not the most exciting. It was a touchdown apart in score, but for most of the game, it was not that close. It was dominated by UGA, but Tech had enough to stay within one TD to the end.

What made it the best is that we were the decided underdogs. 7 points. Tech was the ACC division champ and sported a 10-1 record coming in, ranked 7th at the time. They would go on to win the ACC championship by beating Clemson for the second time that season. The game was in Atlanta.

Ga. had sorely disappointed its fans this year. They opened by losing to Oklahoma State, lost to LSU by a touchdown, then lost to Florida and Kentucky. They beat Auburn and won their bowl. Their record was 6-5 coming in. So, as I mentioned earlier, finishing the season 8-5, while not great, looks a lot better than what it looked like going into *the* game. And let me emphasize, UGA is 6-5 and Tech is 10-1 and is only a touchdown favorite...at home!

Why was this match the most gratifying? For this reason: It was the most important game since Dooley's first in 1964.

After the defeat in 2008, with this game being in Atlanta, with Tech favored, perceived as better and Ga. going nowhere, UGA simply *had* to win this game to prevent a seismic shift in the rivalry. To lose two in a row, even when expected, would have had serious implications. As it was, by winning, it totally changed the future landscape for several years to come. This game was as crucial a game for Ga. as I could remember. Johnson was in his second year and for him to win his first two would have had the same effect as Dooley winning his first two against Dodd. On top of that, Johnson's offense would have gained a lot of credibility.

I dreaded the game the entire week and, while wanting to go, knew I was in for a possibly depressing night! This was much worse than in 1990. Then, Tech was just as good as this year, but Ga. was not. Plus, over that span of time, there emerged a world of difference between the two programs. It was only twenty years chronologically, but it was centuries different in how college football was now being presented to the public. This 2009 Bulldog team had enough talent; it just had not played well. Would they against Tech? Who knew? Plus, we did not have the services of the greatest receiver in UGA history, A.J. Green.

We had seats in the upper deck, with other UGA fans, in the south end zone. It was a good view but cold. They said it was 48 degrees at game time, but up there I think it was about 30.

Tech comes out strutting to the loudest PA system I have ever heard. It was offensive, not to exaggerate. The noise level kept up all night, between plays, at timeouts and all halftime. I heard later that it was mentioned on TV, and they have since toned it down. I know in 2011 and 2013 it was not as bad.

I am thinking as the game starts, *One minute at a time, win most minutes, hang in there, keep the ball* (we all knew that was required) *and keep momentum away from Tech.* My son and I are in a mood that I cannot ever recall being in before; maybe when playing against other teams, yes, but certainly not when playing against Tech. I really feared an embarrassment but, again, feared that a Tech win would mean so much more this year.

The game starts good, UGA runs and runs and runs the ball. There are no throws; it's just a ground game. Defense looks good and holds Tech to 3 points in the first half! Incredible performance. In the first quarter alone, each team had the ball twice but really only once with any meaning, as the other two were at the end of quarters and for three plays.

The defensive coordinator for Ga. had come under a lot of heat and would be let go after the season, but he had them ready for this game. Even with that, everyone knew Tech would score some in the second half. How much they would score, and how much we would score, was the question. All in all, at halftime, I felt that, while so far so good and very proud of the effort, I wasn't sure if they could hold up for 30 more minutes. In football, how many games do you see the underdog play great and then give out? That happens because they expend everything they had and do not have enough talent to go forward when they get tired. Talent eventually wins out.

The half ended in controversy. Tech had the ball with 2 seconds left and with dozens of yards to go for the first down. They run a play, the clock is ticking, and UGA players run off the field thinking Tech will let it run out. Instead, Tech calls timeout with 2 seconds left. The UGA players have to come back out of the locker room to line up for one play. Classless act. At the end of the half, here are some of the stats: UGA, 208 yards rushing; Tech, 80. WOW! It was 17-3, UGA at halftime.

The second half starts, Tech gets the ball, and in one minute and a half, they score on a short pass followed by a missed tackle and a long run. There it is:17-10. Tech is storming back, just like the year before.

Except this year, we get the ball on the ensuing kick-off and on the first play from scrimmage, Caleb King bursts through the Tech line and runs 75 yards for a touchdown! It is the biggest play of the game so far. The mood swing is steep and intense, much like the '78 game when Woerner scored on a punt return and then Tech scored on the ensuing kickoff. This time, however, it was in our favor. That play made you think they could trade punches with Tech and survive. Tech only has 149 yards rushing through three quarters.

Ga. would kick two more field goals in the half and Tech scored two more touchdowns. Tech never caught up or took the lead. Several times they had a chance. Tech closed to 24-17. Then Walsh kicks another field goal and another. Tech is now down 30-17. They do score again and Ga. gets the ball with 7:13 to go, deep in their own territory and up by six. They move it into Tech territory and miss a field goal with 3:07 to go in the game. Tech is now in a do-or-die position.

They move the ball running, but they start to pass since they are running out of time and time outs. They are all vertical down field passes, nothing intermediate. We are holding our breath; it's so close. Would we lose here in the end? But one of the flaws in Johnson's system shows through here. They do not have an intermediate passing game. They did not have to try to get 30 yards at a time, but those are all the plays they had. They had time to complete several intermediate passes and move down the field. We hold after they drop a pass on fourth down.

I have never been prouder of a team and its effort.

Two backs over 150 each...Caleb King and Washaun Ealey. Eight possessions... three TDs, three field goals and one turnover, one running out the clock. Whatever Joe Cox did or did not accomplish in his one year as a starter, this will go down as a feather in his cap.

Again, I have never been prouder of a victory than I am of this 2009 victory over the #7 ranked, 10-1 Tech team! The ACC champion cannot even beat a mediocre Ga. team, a mid-level one in the SEC. It certainly stopped whatever crowing Tech would have undertaken if they had won.

2010

THIS WAS THE WORST YEAR ever under Mark Richt. It saw a losing record, pitiful play, long losing streaks, and the start of serious chatter for his dismissal. They win a lower case game, then lose four in a row. Aaron Murray is the freshman starting quarterback, and it is rough. Then they win three in a row, which was honestly a function of schedule more than anything else, although they were playing better. They couldn't play much worse.

They lose a heartbreaker to Florida and then a real heartbreaker to eventual #1 Auburn and their felonious quarterback, Cam Newton.

So they enter the Tech game, in Athens, 5-6.

Tech, as defending conference champions, enters the game 6-5. Tech loses 42-34. They lose their bowl game to Air Force and wind up 6-7. How Johnson was not put on notice, I will never know. It's just the difference in expectations at the two schools, I guess. On the other hand, maybe he was, and it was not leaked out. Tech has always been good at keeping things close to the vest, "in the family." That's easy to do when your in-state alumni number less than ½ million versus more than a million. And again, after a great year, there was a predicted "down" year the next. It happens most of the time and is unexplainable.

The game is what you would guess: two poor teams slugging it out. Looking at the score, it looks to be exciting, and I guess in a way, it is. But a game with no defense and offenses that are scoring only because of that poor defense is not really a classic game.

It is a night game, but the weather is not bad.

Ga. fumbles the opening kickoff, but Tech does not score. As a matter-of-fact, Georgia gets out to a 14-0 lead at the end of the first quarter. Tech scores twice, and Georgia scores one more time for a 21-14 halftime lead.

In the third quarter, Tech scores as does Georgia and again on a turnover, for a 35-21 lead going into the fourth quarter.

Tech scores to narrow the lead, and they score again with 4:57 to go in the game. For some reason they go for two…and fail. Georgia gets the ball and marches down and scores with 1:29 left on the clock. Tech emulates a "Coach Steve Spurrier" move and lays down for the last score by Washaun Ealy.

Tech gets the ball back and is moving but throws an interception with seconds to go.

Tech had the ball for 38 minutes compared to UGA's 21; they had 512 total yards to UGA's 425; they had 4 turnovers to UGA's 2; and they had a rusher, Allen, rush for 166 yards to our tandem of the year before, King and Ealy's total of less than 160.

But they lose and cannot figure out why.

My take on it is the same old story of expectations where the programs are going and the dominance of attitude. Again, in football, even more so than in basketball (and not at all in baseball), what you believe can carry you so very far…further than your talent level, further than the breaks of the game, further than whether or not you are technically outplayed. When there is an upset between any two teams, it is really an upset because all these variables were overcome.

This game sounds like it was exciting and, as I said, in a way it was. But the level of play was so poor it was hard to be proud of.

Things are not in a good place for the program—too many off-field problems, too many embarrassments, too many transfers. The list can go on. But at least we beat Tech, and that counts for a lot. That's two in a row after losing to Johnson in his first year.

2011

IT'S ANOTHER WEIRD YEAR, but one that winds up mostly happy. Georgia starts the season at the Georgia Dome by losing to Boise State in a bad way. Then the next week they lose to South Carolina, in Athens. They are 0-2! This after going 6-7 the previous year. They have lost three in a row counting last year's bowl loss to Central Florida.

Then a very weird thing occurs. Now understand, the Dawgs are loaded with talent, according to everyone, including the people at the University. That is what makes this so maddening and confusing. The weird part? They proceed to win ten in a row and capture the Eastern Division crown. The tenth win is against Tech—31-17, in Atlanta. This is a credit to Richt and his staff, that they could get the team to pull this winning streak off.

We are down low in the Georgia seats in the west stands. I am optimistic, but deep down there is the remembrance of the start of the year. With it being the Tech game, I wonder which Georgia team will show up.

Tech, meanwhile, comes in 8-3. Again, it's another good record leading into the last few games. They started the season 6-0 and also beat #6 Clemson later. But in between, they lose three games they could have won. With their subsequent bowl loss, they finish 8-5—a very Jim Donnan type of year. It's a good record on paper, but upon closer analysis, you see they did not win any important games, save one.

The game is not close, and Georgia's defense throttles Tech score-wise, which is what you hope for. Let them get their yards, and keep them out of the end zone. The Dawg's offense is clicking. Murray throws the ball at will all over the field. Looking back, this is when they really start to click in Bobo's offense, and from there on, Murray is unquestionably the best passing quarterback in the conference for the next two years. As you may know, he winds up his career with the most yards and many other records in the history of the league. It's kind of hard to believe due to the lack of hype and conference success, but it happened.

The game is essentially over by early in the third quarter. We sit back, relax and savor the scene of beating Tech at Grant Field. It is always more enjoyable to win on the road. Yes, the home crowd is great during a win, but there is nothing like winning at the other guy's place—seeing their faces and hearing their silence. Plus, and I may say this again, Tech has not won at Grant Field since the 1999 game, and that was a rob job. Before that, it was 1989. That's only twice in 22 games.

2012

THIS SEASON IS ONE OF THE STRANGEST ever. Tech goes into the rivalry game 6-5, yet they are the ACC Division champs due to several teams ahead of them not being eligible for the championship game or declining to play! They back in from a fourth place on-the-field finish, record-wise. At one point in the season, they are 3-5.

Georgia, on the other hand, is having an extraordinary season. They lose only to #6 South Carolina in Columbia. I know, it gets old, but it is what it is. Ga. was #5 at the time; they get stomped. No excuse.

They do beat #3 Florida and demolish Ole Miss and Auburn. They come to Athens against Tech 10-1. They win 42-10. We are in our seats with my grandson and son, and—believe it or not—I am worried before the game. I am talking with Sonny Seiler and he says not to worry, Ga. has too much "ass" for Tech. Not sure what he meant, but it sounded good! He was right of course—whatever he meant!

Then, as you may know, we go to the championship game and play eventual national champion Alabama even but lose in the last second on their 10-yard line. We beat Nebraska in the bowl for a 12-2 season. Tech beats Southern California, after losing to FSU in their "championship" game to finish with a 7-7 record. Yes, they went to a bowl with a losing record!

Back to Athens in November.

It is an overcast night, but not too cold. As you might suspect from the score, there was not a lot of drama or closeness in the play. We have so many stars—Jarvis Jones, Aaron Murray, Alec Olgetree, and on and on. The mismatch is blatant and overwhelming.

This is two straight years where Georgia has dominated, regardless of the type of season Tech may have had. To me, and from what I heard from many Tech fans also, the "spread" in talent and resultant outcomes is becoming alarming, and it's one that appears to be impossible to overcome under Johnson.

Nevertheless, Tech keeps Johnson and we head into the 2013 season. Let's see what happens.

But let me repeat: Tech is ACC Division champ, one way or the other, yet the Division champ in the SEC beats them 42-10. Repeat…Ten points for that vaunted offense of Tech's. It's such a clear indication of the talent spread.

2013

THIS GAME IS EERILY SIMILAR to 1978. First let me set the scene—"get the picture," as someone we all know used to say.

It is at night, cold and a little windy, and we are in the very last row in the upper deck on the west side on about the ten-yard line with Georgia fans. There are a smattering of Tech fans also, including one sitting next to me, but I did not know that at the beginning. It was my son, my grandson, and me. I had just gotten back from spending Thanksgiving in Italy with friends and had landed in Atlanta on Thursday evening. (I built in an extra travel day in case there were problems! I could not miss *the* game! More on Italy later.)

Georgia enters the game on a "down" note from, for us, a disappointing season. Tech enters 7-4, (And guess what? Again they lose their last two, losing to Ole Miss in the bowl game.) and they finish the season 7-6. We finish 8-5 and the season unfolds thusly.

We are fifth in pre-season and go to Clemson and throw them the game. I do not mean that in a betting sense but simply in our sloppy play, especially by Murray, who threw a lot of interceptions. We lose players to injury and lose by three points; two missed field goals were among the transgressions.

Then we come home and beat S. Carolina and LSU and with another victory are on a 3-1 roll.

With the hardest schedule in the conference, if not the country, we now play Missouri…and lose. UGA comes out flat after all these tough encounters, and by the time they start playing up to their capabilities, they are behind by too much. They close to within a score but then give up more scores. There were more injuries also, this time to Todd Gurley.

Then they go to Vandy and lose to them in a horrendous exhibition of football.

Then they right the ship for a spell and go to Auburn...again (a scheduling quirk brought about by the conference expansion). This is yet another edition of an Auburn team with either convicted felons or persons charged with crimes populating their roster. They are undefeated under a former Ga. player at quarterback. We play them even, and then one of the most damning sequences I have ever seen unfolds. Murray marches them down the field for a score with seconds to go. Ga. goes ahead. (Auburn is #1 and undefeated, mind you!) Murray scores by bowling over Auburn players at the goal line. I cannot recall ever seeing a quarterback do what he did. He earned my eternal respect on that play. Then the luckiest play ever unfolds by Auburn. Enough said.

We thus come to the Tech game in Atlanta. We are 7-4, same as Tech at that point, and after two straight years in the conference championship game, this is "all" we have left.

Georgia came out playing like that. Tech shoots out to a 20-0 score late into the second quarter. By the way, did I mention we lost Murray to a season-ending injury in the prior game against Kentucky? Hutson Mason is now our quarterback. We are off to a very slow start on offense and are getting killed by the pass from Tech. You read me right—the pass! No excuse. It will be Todd Grantham's last Tech game.

Then we start to click. Ga. scores late in the second quarter from a drive that started on their own 14. I tell my son Clay that this has a feeling eerily familiar to the '78 game. The guy next to me questions what I am referring to. I am much older than him, so I fill him in.

Earlier he asked if I thought Ga. could come back. I told him "not the way they are playing now. They need to get a stop and score...amazing what one simple score can do to a team's psyche."

So it is 20-7, Tech, at halftime. Heck, it was 17-0 with 2 minutes left in the first quarter.

We start the second half scoring ten points to close to 20-17 by the close of third quarter. Even though it is obvious Tech can win, I am starting to get that comfortable feeling of knowing Ga. has "too much ass" for Tech to overcome. Once you feel and see that the Dawgs are in control, they usually stay in control.

Then in the fourth quarter, Tech scores again to get a ten-point lead. At that point, during the TV time-out and with the teams on the field for the kick-off, the Tech players are dancing and acting like they have won the game. Pointing to their fans and clapping, pointing to us and making all sorts of unprintable gestures. The time on the clock reads 10:34. I will never forget that scene—such arrogance, such lack of discipline, such lack of maturity. Typical Tech.

So what happens? Forever gratefully, Georgia scores at the six-and-one-half minute mark to draw within three. They had a fourth and six inside their own territory with nine-and-one-half minutes to go in the game, and they convert, moving to midfield! This play and this drive is when the game was won.

Tech now gets the ball deep in their own territory....We intercept! They hold, to their credit, and we kick a tying field goal with seconds on the clock. Overtime...again.

At this point, I am aware that the guy sitting next to me is in fact a Tech fan! He is mad! I am going on about how this team, Georgia, is coached differently than the Tech team. He does not understand. Then I realize his prior questions were more of a nature of "will they" not "can they."

Tech gets the ball first in overtime and scores. Georgia gets the ball and scores...Well, Gurley scores by carrying the ball on every play.

Then, according to the rules, we get the ball first in the second overtime. On the first play, Gurley bursts through and runs 25 yards for a score. Tech gets the ball and we hold, batting down the last play, a pass in the end zone.

Georgia wins! 41-34.

That sequence of plays is so quick, really, that we are almost stunned at the suddenness of the victory. I feel like I did in the '71 game...sheer exhaustion but sheer excitement also. This becomes one of the classics, no doubt! I have mentioned here and said many times that these kinds of games are the best to win. The look on the opponent's face, the fans (being there, as I have said, creates this opportunity), the looks of pure shock are worth so many memories. To take a game away from a team at the last second is a feeling better than crushing them, in my opinion. To do it to Tech is the height. To do it at their field is icing on the cake, a very *big* cake!

This game is so much like that '78 game (not including the overtime, which did not exist at the time). Tech with an early 20-0 lead; Ga. scoring with 42 seconds left (in '13) in the half to cut the lead; Ga. scoring in the third quarter to catch up; Tech getting back ahead and then Ga. scoring late to win. How sweet it is!

A word on Todd Gurley: all throughout most of the game it was obvious he was still not recovered from the injury earlier in the season. But when it counted, he came through. He rushed for 122 yards. More on him in the next year.

Mason, from the middle of the second quarter on, settled down and looked every bit the part of a Georgia quarterback.

2014

THIS GAME REMINDS YOU that each year, each game is separate, and you should enjoy each one on its own merits. You never know what will follow!

I truly believe in sports where you "pay for" games that are won, like the one in 2013. Or, on the negative side, you pull one out for a previous bad one. (See Auburn during the time we are talking about here!) It's superstitious, yes, but it seems to hold nonetheless. A yin and yang to life, especially in sports, does exist.

This is one of those games that UGA should have won going in, should have won while playing it, and should have won when it was over, but instead they beat themselves. Of course, you could make the case that they should have lost based on all the bad plays they made, but the score is what counts and they had the advantage when it counted. Now hear this: they were outplayed and *out-coached*. They had more talent, so, even when playing average, they still are in the game with Tech.

This game was evenly matched only because UGA made it so. It was one of the most exciting games in history. The only trouble for us was that UGA lost. I think it will make Tech's top ten all-time games but not ours.

Tech won, in the second straight overtime game, 30-24. The way it transpired reminded me of a couple of those games under Donnan. On at least three different occasions UGA literally handed the ball to Tech to win. Tech did the same thing twice. Then you factor in a couple of other plays, and it is easy to see why UGA lost. Let me say here (and this is hard to say not because it is the truth but because of the implications) Tech outhustled, outsmarted and outplayed UGA, play for play. *Still,* the Bulldogs could have and should have won the damn game! Tech deserved to win, but Georgia was in a position to steal yet another win. Yet, like I said, they beat themselves. After all is said and done, yes, Tech won, but Ga. had so many opportunities and ways to win. Tech had nothing to do with Ga. coming out and, while playing well execution-wise, making too many self-inflicted mistakes. Tech had nothing to do with bad decisions by the coaching staff. Tech had nothing to do with fate. That reminds me of an old saying, "I do not have to be great, just better than you." That has only happened twice since I have been going to these games. Tech got 90% of all the breaks in the game. Breaks, if you want to call them that, were simply the times where they were in a position to win. Regardless, there were two fumbles not caused by Tech, two stupid player decisions, and two stupid coaching decisions. Then Ga. does two things that they have never done before. More on those later.

The weather was great and for the third straight year I, along with my youngest son and his son, sat in our season ticket seats. The day before was an ominous start. Ga. needed Arkansas to beat Missouri for UGA to be division champs. They did not. That meant Ga. was playing for pride and positioning for bowls and rankings, nothing else. This is a team that had to face a lot of adversity, and much of it was of their own making. The great Todd Gurley only played six games. Up to this game they lost only twice, but the losses are to 6-6 South Carolina and Florida—no excuse for that. They could have easily been undefeated. But there is always something that happens that derails the possibility.

Tech has had a good year also. They have two losses to two mediocre teams also, but they squeeze out a division title when no one expected that. For the millionth time, though, Ga. had a better team and should have won at home. Ga. was outplayed; I may say that several more times here. There is absolutely no excuse for that to happen.

We started the game great, like a locomotive, taking the opening kickoff and marching right down the field for a touchdown. Ga. held Tech scoreless into the second quarter, but in that general span of time, they fumbled on two different drives at Tech's one-yard line. Tech does score later. Tech is ready to score again with all momentum on their side, when we strip the ball from the ball carrier, the quarterback, at our one-yard line, and Damien Swann races 99 yards for a touchdown! It's 14-7, Georgia. Halftime. Want to call that a "break?" Ok, I give you that one, and I take the other three by Tech.

In the third quarter, Tech holds the ball for about 11 minutes and scores to tie. Then the fourth quarter starts. Oh, I forgot to mention, we fake a punt for a first down. We block a field goal attempt; they block a field goal attempt. There's a lot of "noise, " but neither team is getting the upper-hand points-wise. By this time, however, with the fourth quarter now upon us and the Tech offense holding the ball for so long, I am *worried*.

We eventually go up 17-14. Tech scores and goes up 21-17 in the fourth quarter with not much time left. They kick off a punch kick, and we watch it fall between two of our players while Tech recovers the ball. It was one of those "Are you kidding me?" moments. It was one of those times in sports (you know them, I'm sure) when you give "that look" to someone as if to ask, "Is this the twilight zone?" Tech is driving with under three minutes to go. All is lost. They have the ball, the lead and the clock on their side.

It's the next play…and they *fumble*! We recover! We march right down the field under the direction of the best drive Mason has ever engineered all year (pun intended!) to score with 18 seconds left. It's now 24-21, UGA! At this point, I feel ecstatic, but I have an additional feeling of being unsettled. With this score and the time left, I should have felt as if the game was now finally won. But sometimes I get these funny feelings, and they concern me. I got one here and, as we shall see, it was correct.

We squib kick, courtesy of Coach Richt, and they return to their 45. They have no timeouts left. I am really uneasy now! Tech has time for one play and a field goal attempt. The quarterback scrambles from a pass play and runs to UGA's 35.These were two horrible plays that exhibited both coaching errors and player errors.

There were four seconds left. They have to attempt a 53-yard field goal—the longest in their kicker's career. I *still* do not feel like we will win. I am worried because if there is a play left to be had, then it is a play that can beat you.

The kick hits the crossbar…and *gets over*…Overtime! Some pictures that were taken show a UGA player's fingertips a centimeter away from the ball, if not brushing it. So close!

Oh, I forgot to add: they were scrambling to get the kicking team on the field and were running out of play clock when Richt calls a time out!

This is the first overtime game in the history of Sanford Stadium! And we have to lose to Tech. It's the second straight overtime game in series.

They get the ball first in overtime and score, but we block the extra point! We are supposed to feel like fate is on our side and we will win. But how many chances can we be given?

We get the ball and are driving with a second and goal on the nine.

We pass…

They intercept…

Game over….

Tech wins….

The crowd is silent—even Tech's side was silent since it was so sudden…

Then Tech players go wild…

We go home.

We were so close to ripping their hearts out again, which I always contend is the best of victories, and this time they thwart it. It reminds me of the 1999 game, but this one was much worse. This is absolutely the worst feeling ever in a Tech game for me. There is not another game in this streak that matches this one for a UGA fan. They never ripped our hearts out at the last second like they did here. It was so numbing. It was weeks later when it sunk in completely, and the hurt became intense. Even 1998 and 1999 were not like this. The euphoria felt when you are on the winning side is the best feeling…and when you are on the losing side, it is the worst.

Dang 'em. Wait 'till next year.

Speaking of next year, I will say right now (written at the end of 2014) that I fear losing Mike Bobo, Tony Ball, and others will have serious, negative repercussions. I stand to be corrected if I'm wrong, and we will know by the time this is published. I gave this manuscript to a number of people to look at, and they can vouch that I had this in 2014. See the section on 2015.

Meanwhile, Mike Bobo takes a team at Colorado State that had been up and down, and they win seven games, finish second in the conference and go to a bowl.

UGA goes on to beat Louisville, Petrino the Terrible, and Grantham the Vagabond in a bowl, while Tech demolishes Mississippi State. We finish ranked 8th and Tech is 7th. It's quite an amazing end to a season. If only it were reversed, it would have been better. But I have to admit that having the top two schools in the state finish next to each other in the top ten is, I think, unprecedented.

I have one last thought on this game, I promise. Tech wins, for the first time in six games and the second time in 14 games. Tech starts talking about the shift in momentum. "The 2015 team can contend for a national championship." "We (Tech) now have the upper hand." Statements like these are what galls me no end. Even if Tech was clearly superior and won going away, those statements would not be true. They clearly do not understand the dynamics of a rivalry in a sports setting. Win one game and they go crazy, thinking that means all is well. Can you imagine what it was like when they did win most of the time? One win does not a winning streak make, nor does it mean a shift in dominance. And, I assure you, winning at the clip UGA has in these past fifteen years *is* dominance.

2015

MY CLOSING STATEMENT at the end of the 2014 recap about the coaching changes has been proven correct. More on that later.

As for my streak, this game, as it turned out, was going to be the most difficult for me to attend, even many months out, not counting last minute occurrences that can wreck a plan. (No pun intended.) My wife and I moved to Italy for a six-month sabbatical in early August, with plans to come back in February. Well, many people, including my sons, asked, "what was I going to do about the Tech game?" When around the female species, eyes would roll and they would say, "I just do not understand that," "Really, are you crazy?" I told them, of course, that I am planning to come back for the game.

So, I had to get an "in-between" ticket to fly back on Thanksgiving and fly back to Italy on that following Sunday. A friend's wife, asked, "If this was the 51st game, would you have done this?" After a long pause, I said, "You know, I just may not have," and I let it rest at that.

Alas, as it turned out, while nothing could stop me in Georgia, I could not overcome international law. Or rather, I did not choose to challenge international law. Here is what happened. We went to Italy, but because we were to stay six months, we had to get a special Visa. However, we did not do that because my wife and I would have had to go to Miami, Florida to get the Visa at the Italian Embassy. We simply could not do that. So we took our chances, and when we got to Italy, we did all sorts of research. We found out that leaving Italy for the U.S. and then come back to Italy was chancy. It would depend on the passport official at the booth in Rome and/or in Atlanta. It was too much of a risk. If I had been "flagged," I would or could have been prevented from going back to Italy and rejoining my wife for the final two months of our trip! It was too big of a chance. If it was just me, I would have chanced it, but I could not do it with those higher stakes!

So, with one game to go before getting to fifty straight, the streak *ended*! As I mentioned regarding earlier references, life is bigger than a game or a rivalry. It was disappointing, but when put in context, it was really no choice at all. Rather, it was only a gamble, with the odds stacked against me. Also, 49 straight is pretty good, and what is fifty? Fifty out of fifty-one, or even fifty-one out of fifty-two, is really just as good. It was sad, though, having the game played without me being there. How could they have done that?

I am happy to report my son and his son went. My son now has 33 straight and his son, three straight. (Well...he is only six!)

BACK TO THE GAME.

The coaching changes were a disaster. There were so many negative feelings, some negative press coverage, and such lack of effort on the field. All this can mean only one thing when a team underperforms like this one did: dissension. I have never seen it worse, not in 1974, 1977, 1993, or 1994.

But I listened to the game on the radio, as I did the entire year while in Italy. What can be said about two of the worst teams in this series? I say worst not based on the records (though Tech's was pretty bad) but because they both underachieved, they both had much worse records than predicted, and, most of all, both showed a baffling lack of desire. Nevertheless, the game has to be played. The score was13-7 favoring UGA. While it is fair to say the game was not that close, it is also accurate to say neither team played well. Any single play could have happened that could have changed the eventual outcome.

Their two seasons went like this. Georgia beat one team with a winning record and lost badly to the two teams they needed to beat, or at least play well enough against to be within range of beating. In the Alabama and Florida games, they did not even show up. Tech beat two teams in Division I. One was on a fluke, which is very hard to believe, and if you would have stated that before the season, you would have been labeled a heretic! So, as I said, this game really was unlike any other that I can remember.

Georgia scored early on, in an attempt to convert a fourth down and also with one from Tech's 30, and they held Tech scoreless through over three quarters of the game. As a matter of fact, Tech was about to punt when Georgia gave them a penalty, which resulted in a first down which they used to keep possession and score. Georgia had an advantage in some statistics, including time of possession, but mostly you got the feeling that Tech would be hard-pressed to score, more so than Georgia, who had a pitiful offense of their own. Georgia had one of its best offensive outputs all year, and I will be the first to say that their offense was below average. Tech's defense is that bad. It will be interesting to see what Johnson does about his situation.

The weather was great, the crowd was mediocre (according to my son), and the teams played as they had all year—Tech with turnovers, a lack of third down conversions, and an average defense; UGA with a sub-par quarterback, below-par offensive line blocking, and an amazing ability to go to sleep for long periods.

It is now 20 hours after the above was written, and I now inject the storyline of the end of the Richt era. It is not the subject of this memoir to expound on him from a personal viewpoint or to elaborate on the event of his leaving. This is about the games themselves and not the occurrences surrounding them.

I will say this one thing to emphasize a point: something had to be done. Just witness all I wrote about that had gone wrong. That usually can be traced back to the head coach. The program simply could not continue on the track it had been on for the previous six to eight years, winning meaningless games and losing almost all the important ones that counted against teams with winning records.

I have one last thought. As I have hinted at in this writing, the standards and expectations at Tech and UGA are so different. Tech goes 3-9 and finishes their fourth lackluster season out of the last five—Johnson stays and is praised. UGA goes 9-3, but continues to beat nobody of consequence, as well as lose to some they should have beaten—Richt is let go.

OBSERVATIONS AND STATISTICS

HERE ARE A FEW reflections and some statistics to show the breadth and depth of the series.

Until Vince Dooley arrived, the all-time series record was 26-25-5 in favor of Georgia. Now it is 65-38-5—So say we, Dawgs. Tech says it's 65-40-5. Either way, UGA is ahead by a lot.

Since 1964, Georgia has compiled a 39-13 record; since I started going, a 37-13 record. This computes a 75% and a 73% winning clip for the Dawgs. Another way to say it is that Georgia lost 26% of the games. For comparison, the Auburn-Alabama, Michigan-Ohio State, USC-UCLA, Texas-Oklahoma, Princeton-Harvard rivalries of long standing are usually more competitive than ours.

Of the 13 games Georgia has lost, only five have been in Atlanta, eight have been in Athens! That, to me, is an anomaly. A team that dominates a series that much overall, who wins 75% of the time yet loses most (61%) of the games they lose, are at home, is irrational.

Let me elaborate on this. Here we are in 2015. The last time Tech won at home was in 1999! And that was, roundly agreed by all, a farce due to a ref's call. Then before that, it was in 1989! Before that, it was 1985. Then 1977. And before that, 1970. Wow! Two victories in a twenty-nine-year period, in thirty games, and in fifteen games at home! So that means Tech won three times at their place in twenty-two games prior to that. That is yet another indicator of how they have become less competitive.

Another measurement is this: there is not one class at Tech who won all four years since the fifties. There are a number of those classes at UGA! Another way to describe this series from a Dawg viewpoint is that there are only three games—1974, 1990 and 2000—where I felt, well before the end of the game, that we had lost. So, even when defeat occurs, it does not seem to be such until the final horn sounds.

By decade, the series looks like this.

1960-69	'70-'79	'80-'89	'90-'99	'00-'09	'10-'15
6-4	7-3	7-3	7-3	8-2	5-1
VD-5-1	VD	VD-7-2	RG-5-1	MR-8-1	MR-5-1
		RG-0-1	JD-2-2	JD-0-1	

VD= Vince Dooley RG=Ray Goff MR= Mark Richt JD-Jim Donnan

It's amazingly consistent from decade to decade, until we hit the 21st century, when Mark Richt takes over. Maybe that's when the disparity I have talked about takes hold. Disparity is caused by so many factors—some mentioned here, some to be mentioned later and some just overlooked. Whichever theory you subscribe to, the gap has widened. A number of games are close, but Georgia wins almost all of them. I have mentioned several measurements that provide clues as to why. By way of elaboration, let me be specific. With the growth of the state, the growth of revenue from TV, the growth of the university's student population, the success of UGA's athletic programs versus Tech's and, lastly, with the number of well-to-do alumni of UGA who still have connections in the state of Georgia, the amount of money in each athletic fund is more divergent than ever, by tens of millions of dollars. Georgia now has more and better facilities and "incidentals" which enhance their efforts in athletics.

Tech has the longest winning streak—eight, compiled in the fifties. Georgia has come close several times, but has not matched it, much less broken it. Given my age, I do not know if I will ever see it broken.

Starting in my first year, 1966, I will recount the years Tech won when they were favored, as well as those when they were favored and lost. I will also do the same regarding UGA games By "favored" here, I mean more by the pundits than the bookies—you know, with betting being illegal and all that! Keep in mind, when you only win 13 times in half a century, there are not many examples of being favored and winning.

Tech+=won	Tech+=lost	UGA+=won	UGA+=lost
1970	1966	1967, 1968	1969
1990	2009	1971, 1972	1974
2000 (P)	1991	1973, 1975	1977
	2001	1976, 1978	1984
		1979, 1980	1989
		1981, 1982	1998
		1983, 1985	2008
		1986, 1987	2014
		1988, 1992	1999
		1993, 1994	
		1995, 1996	
		1997, 2002	
		2003, 2004	
		2005, 2006	
		2007, 2010	
		2011, 2012	
		2013, 2015	

As I mentioned before, winning streaks are lopsidedly in favor of Georgia. Georgia lost three in a row once during this period and never more than that. When you consider that they only lost 13 times, you think losing three in a row means they hardly lost "in a row" at all, but the contrary is actually true. In a factoid labeled "Stranger Than Fiction," Georgia loses two in a row, three different times. That, combined with the three in a row from 1998 to 2000, adds up to nine of their thirteen wins. This constitutes a winning streak for Tech. Maybe that is why they get so excited when they win—they know there is a possibility of another. When they lose, on the contrary, they know more losses are to follow. Anyway, it seems that when Tech wins, they do it in bunches—*very* small bunches, but bunches nonetheless.

And here's another observation on this series: coaches.

Georgia has had only a handful since before WWII…Butts, Griffith, Dooley, Goff, Donnan, Richt and now Smart. Before that, there had been a number of them, and Tech never missed an opportunity to remind everyone.

What do I mean?

Going back to just before the mid-20th century, Tech had had a handful of coaches themselves, then Dodd retired in 1966. Bobby Dodd coached at Tech longer than anyone, almost as long as Dooley at Georgia. Dodd, 18 years; Dooley, 25 years. But when Dodd retired, the revolving door started. Since Dodd left there have been—count 'em—*nine* coaches at Georgia Tech. The transition from a legend at Tech did not go as smoothly as they wanted. In the past fifty-three years, Dooley and Richt have been the coaches for forty of those years!

Best Games.

I mentioned several times the old argument about what type of game is the best: a blow-out, or a thriller with maybe a come-from-behind victory. It's the game that's won when you are the underdog, or a game where there's a big win and you were favored to have it. I have gone back and forth on this, and in grand political style I have decided that *both* can be viewed as "the best." Here are the ones I rate as the top ten and the reasons why. As you will see, "best" means several things.

First, I want to reference an Honorable Mention: 1966, 23 to 14. I'm not mentioning it because it is my first game but because it is Coach Bobby Dodd's last game. I did not realize such at the time, but this is significant. Add to it the fact that both teams are ranked in the top ten for one of the very few times in their history. Tech is undefeated and therefore in the running for a national championship and being televised (regionally). These are all reasons for it being a very significant game. UGA wins with some ease, but the game itself is huge at that time and, looking back, it still is.

Number 10:1968, 47 to 8. This makes the list because it is the second worst beating during this period and, I think, the third worst in history. This Georgia team was undefeated (with two ties) and it was the first game I went to by myself. I luxuriated in the warmth of the game (it was cold and dreary, actually, weather-wise) and remember to this day that this is what it feels like to stomp someone of note.

Number 9: 1995, 18 to 17. This is Goff's last regular season game, and it is a thriller in that Ga. is behind and mounts a field-long drive to kick a winning field goal with less than a minute left. The adversity of this game, this season and this coach make this a melodrama of the highest order. To come back and score to win late was poetic.

Number 8: 2001, 31 to 12. This game is not a thriller in the score or in the playing of the game, nor is it a blow-out. It is listed because it broke a three-game losing streak. Going in, no matter the season records and who was favored, you had the feeling, as a three-time loser, that it might happen again. This was a game of huge significance. There was a huge sigh of relief when it was in the bag—a great feeling made even more special because it was at Grant Field. It was "must-win" game for UGA and for the new coach, Mark Richt.

Number 7: 1991, 18 to 15. (Same reason as #8.) This is coming off the national championship year for Tech, coming after a two-year losing streak and being at Tech. It was Goff's first of five straight victories against Tech, as he had lost his first two. It was a great feeling when Hearst broke a long one and you knew then that UGA was headed to victory. Getting a victory when there is a real need for one is very special. We won by "only" three, but it felt much larger.

Number 6: 1975, 42 to 26. This is one of my all-time favorites. At Grant Field. At night (and freezing at that). And the fact that we jumped to a 42-0 lead. Wow. But most of all, it makes the list because it comes after the absolutely worst defeat in history, the 1974 debacle in Athens, in the sleet. The intensity, the desire, the hatred (sorry, that is what I felt at the time and so did many of my friends there with me) was so palpable that if Georgia did not jump to such a big lead, I don't know what we fans would have done. Obviously, the team felt the same way and the players embarrassed Pepper. Then they let their foot off the pedal some to make it closer than it really was, score-wise. But, no two ways about it, it was a blow-out and much, much more!

Number 5: 2013, 41 to 34. This is the second overtime game when our great running back Todd Gurley is half-speed and Mark Richt is under fire. We are at Grant Field and Tech plays well. But as is the case with Tech, when they get on top, they start to showboat. Then we come back. We have no running game, we have a mediocre quarterback and we are behind by two scores with one quarter to go. But we forge a tie and then win in overtime. A great feeling. It is enhanced by the realization that we played at about 70% while Tech played at 100%, and we still won! *Snatching* a game from Tech that they have, by all rights, won, is a great feeling indeed!

Number 4: 1978, 29 to 28. As with the previous game, we get behind by twenty points in the first half. As in the 2013 game, we score late in the half then come out in the second half and score again to make it a game. My emotions go from absolute depression, to a faint glimmer of hope, to an all-out belief that we will, indeed, win! Then we score late to win, in this case, by going for two to secure the victory. The come-from-behind scenario is great, maybe the best. But this game had a little of everything and it is one of the all-time best. Some may argue that is it *the* best and I would not dispute that, but I have my reasons for the other three just ahead.

Number 3: 1997, 27 to 24. As far as pulling a victory from defeat, this is the all-time best. We have the game won, then Tech scores very late and we are down and out, with virtually no time left. But Tech kicks the ball out-of-bounds, so we get the ball on the 35 (with no time expired from running a kick-off back), and we have a faint hope to win. In just a few seconds Mike Bobo engineers (yes, a pun!) a march of 65 yards to score with no time left. There was pandemonium at Grant Field, at least in two corners of the stadium! It was a victory stolen, and those are great. We have very few, and they do feel good. That is why this is listed here.

Number 2: 1971, 28 to 24. In the greatest year of college football, in the first Tech-Georgia game ever televised nationally, and with one of the greatest UGA teams ever, at Grant Field and in desperation of victory, we get a win in the last seconds. Again, we needed to break a two-game losing streak. The fear of losing a third at their place creates a tension that explodes with relief when it is avoided. This was the first of its kind (a come from behind with little time left) since the fifties, maybe. It was a beautifully executed drive to secure victory. And it was another heartbreak for Tech; I love 'em!

Number 1: 2009, 30 to 24. You can debate them all, but I will not yield on this one. To be the underdog, to have had the season we had, to have lost the year before and to be at Grant Field, to come to the game and know that you are likely to lose (see 1990) and then to see the team come out and start to outplay Tech—play by play, series by series, quarter by quarter—creates emotions that will never be forgotten. In games like these—and we Georgia fans have had *very* few—you dream that this can happen, but it very rarely does. Yet in 2009, it does. We beat Tech. From this game on it is obvious that the two programs are on different planes. Since there are few times we are underdogs, and even fewer when we are big underdogs, to have *everything* be against you and still win this type of game is very special. When UGA had been left for dead (and at that point in time, it had been that way, at most, three times) we came and won this game as few have done. We got thirty points on the ACC champs. It was payback for the previous year and, more importantly, it brought Tech and Paul Johnson back down to earth, where they have stayed ever since.

So those are my Ten Best games—some close, some blow-outs and some of significance beyond the game day itself are all ranked for this period, 1966-2015. You rank yours and, either way, you cannot go wrong!

Now let me wrap up and follow-up on my opening remarks.

I have talked about the difference between the two schools, their fans, their mindset, and the series in general. At this stage of the evolvement of our state, 2016 A.D., as well as the evolvement of these two institutions of the University System of Georgia, the fact is that my prior assessment does not hold anymore. The students at both schools now are so different than they were fifty years ago. (Aren't they everywhere?)

The students at Tech still more closely resemble those in the sixties than those at UGA do. Tech's students have a narrow range of academic interests versus the range of majors at UGA. That makes it easier to "stay the same." I think this is an under-appreciated factor in the differences in the schools. But, make no mistake, there have been changes. The make-up is more international than at the University of Georgia.

The fact is, at one time, the number of students at Tech were more international than they were national or local. This was during the seventies and eighties—there were more out-of-state and out of country students than there were in-state students—but this was "addressed" when state officials complained that Ga. (state of) students, who were scoring just as well, were being passed over for foreign students to be admitted to Tech.

A word about Georgia Tech, the institution. It may seem I have been a little rough on them here, but the fact is that Tech is a great engineering school. One that all Georgians should be proud of. They have a hard time, mostly, in athletics but that does not diminish their academics. I want to make sure that is understood and that I have great respect for them as an institution of higher learning.

Now let me get back to comparisons. Tech students still major in those courses that are offered traditionally at Tech and specialized in there, and that will always attract a certain type student and personality. So, in that regard, they are still similar; now there are just more of them.

At UGA, it is so different now compared to fifty years ago. I debated with myself about how much to write on it; it is that involved. Let's just synopsize it thusly. Most of the students are from greater metro Atlanta. There is very little diversity. The black percentage is much higher than thirty years ago, but it is still nowhere near a Georgia State or Kennesaw State. When you are at 3% (as it was in the early eighties), you have nowhere to go but up. Agriculture and similar subjects are majored in but by very few. Most of the students have parents or grandparents that were not born in the south, let alone in Georgia. This change started in the nineties, some say due to the advent of the HOPE Scholarship. Therefore, UGA is now an elite university, and I am not saying that as a bragging point. I am not even sure I am proud of it at all, because from its beginning until the nineteen-nineties, it was a place where anyone who wanted to go to college and qualified academically could go.

This change has wrought a number of differences in following sports as well as in the tolerance of the coaches and the jobs they do.

The entrance scores of the incoming freshmen at both schools are so much higher than fifty years ago. The view of Tech towards UGA is still a distinct one but for different reasons. Now, however, UGA students look "down" at Tech students also.

One thing has never changed. When Tech loses year after year, it is because of the rigorous academics. When they win, who knows why? I guess the courses got easier...or the athletes got smarter! The fact is, a person inclined to social sciences will not do well in applied aerodynamics and, conversely, a person versed in physics will not do well in political science and applied theory. It's the old "right brain, left brain" theory. Each is hard to that student who is not inclined to that field of study. Nevertheless, it is a relied-upon myth that Tech is a "harder" school than UGA. Maybe it was fifty years ago, but it isn't now.

How does this discussion fit into a narrative on college football? Much of the appeal of this sport is the atmosphere in the community, before the game, in the stadium and after the game. All of that has changed dramatically during this period.

For starters, it is extremely hard to get Tech students to come to the games. It is hard also at UGA—not as hard, but too hard for comfort. This is a problem across the land, even in the South. It happens at places like Alabama, believe it or not, and their coach, Nick Saban, has commented on this phenomenon. (Compare to my opening comments on growing up in the south many years ago.) This would have been inconceivable when I was a little boy!

This is due to the fact that the majority, or at least the plurality, of students are not rooted from the south. There are, of course, other reasons: too many distractions, too costly, too easy to watch on TV (remember my comment about no TV). But the culture in the south has changed.

Second, the connection between these students and the institution is not as it used to be. Allow me to elaborate. Now, students at both schools view their time on campus as being spent to get a degree, which leads them to other endeavors in life. It is not viewed as a place to spend four years of their lives in an institution that is part of the fabric of this state. Don't get me wrong. They *are* there for an education, but it should be more of an integrated experience than one where they "use" the institution and then discard it when they're finished. There are many students that stay "attached" to the school, but there are many more now who do not.

This creates a different dynamic for athletic departments and the coaches. They, too, are now looking for ways to "attract" students into the stadium! It is unbelievable that they have to do that! There is no longer a feeling of being "for" the school and its teams just because it is here in this state.

The game itself is as popular as ever, but being in the stadium is not what it used to be. One reason is, and I may be showing my age here, that it is so hard to get to and from a game now, with the starting times for TV, the large crowds and the traffic that it all brings. Yes, there are 92,000 people in Sanford stadium now. When I started, there were somewhere between 48,000 to 52,000 people. But in 1966, the population of the state was about 3,500,000. Now it is over 10,000,000! The mix of people is different also. This makes for a different attitude in the stands.

Remember when I talked about whether or not the Tech game is the most important for Georgia fans? The fact that we even have to discuss that as being a valid point or not shows how things have changed. Fifty years ago, the discussion would not have even occurred. I believe thirty years from now, maybe sooner, this game *will* be just another on the schedule.

But in my life, and for now, it is still THE *GAME*. And I was lucky enough to see over 40% of them all!

www.ingramcontent.com/pod-product-compliance
Lightning Source LLC
Chambersburg PA
CBHW072350090426

42741CB00012B/2993